98

WILLIAM A. CARTER

D1257322

WILLIAM A. CARTER

CHANNELS
OF
SPIRITUAL POWER

CHANNELS
OF
SPIRITUAL POWER

Frank C. Laubach

FLEMING H. REVELL COMPANY

Copyright, MCMLIV, by

FLEMING H. REVELL COMPANY

Printed in the United States of America

LIBRARY OF CONGRESS CATALOG CARD NUMBER: 54-9684

Westwood, N. J.–316 Third Avenue
Los Angeles 41–2173 Colorado Boulevard
London E. C. 4–29 Ludgate Hill
Glasgow C. 2–229 Bothwell Street

TO

*all who are dissatisfied
with what they are doing
for the world*

Contents

CHANNELS
OF
SPIRITUAL POWER

Lord, make me a *channel* of Thy peace
That where there is hatred—I may bring love,
That where there is wrong—I may bring the spirit of forgive-
ness,
That where there is discord—I may bring harmony,
That where there is error—I may bring truth,
That where there is doubt—I may bring faith,
That where there is despair—I may bring hope,
That where there are shadows—I may bring light,
That where there is sadness—I may bring joy.

Lord, grant that I may seek rather to comfort—than to be
comforted;
To understand—than to be understood;
To love—than to be loved;
for
It is by giving—that one receives;
It is by self-forgetting—that one finds;
It is by forgiving—that one is forgiven;
It is by dying—that one awakens to eternal life.
Amen.

St. Francis of Assisi

I

THE ONLY WAY OUT

HISTORY WILL RECORD THAT FROM 1950 ONWARDS America began to have her greatest religious revival. There is reason to hope that this is the *beginning* of the greatest revival of all time, not only in the United States but throughout the whole world. The latest statistics available show that the churches gained more than twice as many members in 1952 as they had gained in any previous year. The churches grew 2½ times faster than the population. The report of the National Council of Churches called this "a whopping gain of 3,604,124 over the count of 1951." Two thirds of these new members were Protestants and one third were Catholics.

Norman Vincent Peale says that there is a revival among business men. His own astonishing audience, said to be as much as thirty million a week through his radio, television, syndicated newspapers, magazine articles, books and sermons, seems to support his statement. Evangelist Billy Graham has bigger crowds and more penitents than Billy Sunday had in his most impressive years. Bishop Sheen is equally effective in the Roman Catholic Church.

But this American revival is not confined to a few preachers or even to a few hundred preachers. Preaching is not the *cause* of this revival; the preachers whose churches are crowded have merely responded to the real cause. This

11

revival is not produced by men preaching hell fire as Jonathan Edwards and Billy Sunday preached it; a future hell does not scare many people today. *But people are scared about their own world here and now.*

The scientists started this revival, not with sermons but with atom and hydrogen bombs and guided missiles. Newspapers and magazines have stimulated it to the point where they have Americans thoroughly scared about a future war that can destroy every human being in any large city in the world in a matter of seconds. Most of the people of the United States feel like the characters in a murder story when hidden death creeps upon them. This apprehension affects them in a variety of ways. It has driven some people to heavier drinking in an attempt to forget it. And, on the other hand, it is driving millions of others to God and to church.

The popular preachers seldom mention war or bombs; that is the last thing people want to hear in church. They want sermons on "How to get rid of fear and worry," "How to emphasize the positive and eliminate the negative." People are crowding the churches, hoping that somehow their courage and faith and peace of mind may find new support.

This is of tremendous value, but it has one defect. The bomb and the threat still remain, while the "spiritual" tonic wears off in the course of a week. Monday morning's newspaper again confronts us with the statement of some military expert that neither the United States nor Russia has found any defense. In two or three years, perhaps in less time than that, Russia will be able to annihilate the greater part of the people of America within twenty-four hours. We can retaliate and convert most of Russia into a vast Hiroshima. Then some meek little neutral country could have what was left of the world. The scientists and the military men do not *want* us to learn how to live in peace with the hydrogen bomb. Einstein says:

I think the most dangerous thing for us would be to get accustomed to this new danger and try to live along as usual. To live in an armed camp where each threatens to annihilate the other, is simply intolerable.

This bomb hanging over our heads is producing another type of revival among many thousands of our people. When they turn to God they seem to hear Him say: "You ask *me* to save the world from catastrophe. I need *your* help! You must help me to change those evil men who have power to destroy you and your world. I am ready to pour heaven's help on the world, but I need you and multitudes like you to be my channels."

The best measure of the power of this revival lies in determining how many men and women answer "yes" to this call of God, and how many are willing to sacrifice their own plans and interests in order to help. Jesus called on His disciples to take up their cross and follow Him. Swelling church rolls may or may not represent the religion of Jesus.

I crossed the United States during the past few months, asking for men and money to reach out a helping hand to the world's unfortunates. After the services, men and women, young and old, came forward and offered to give *all* of their lives and *all* of their money.

One of these came to see me. He is president of a prosperous engineering company. This is what he said:

I heard you say that in America men and women of large talents devote their efforts to selling gadgets to people who already have too much. This struck home. I have been doing that, and I'm sick of selling people what they do not need when the world is so desperately hungry. I want to devote my engineering skills to helping real need. I do not need any salary; I can support myself.

Hundreds of men and women like this man have become disgusted with wasting their talents on tasks that leave the world no better, and in many cases leave it even worse. They want to consecrate their talents to God and human need. They want to become God's channels.

If this peril continues, the revival will continue, and as it grows, an ever-swelling army of our finest men and women will be increasingly disgusted with prostituting their talents on baubles and will offer themselves to help save the world. Two things will continue to stand out high above all others. First, the unthinkable peril for the world. Second, the uncompromising demand of Jesus Christ to sacrifice self for the cause.

Already the men and women who have offered their all to save their world are giving this revival a nobler quality than any previous revival has ever had. These are the people who are following Christ, not for what they can get here or hereafter, but for what they can do for the world. These are really taking up their cross; they are the true successors of Paul.

But men who have made this great decision find that their problem is not ended the moment they decide. It is only just begun. We are always tempted, as Jesus was, to try some surface short-cut cure which will leave our way of life as little disturbed as possible. But, alas, no surface cure is going to be enough. This world has a deep soul-disease, and nothing short of a drastic change in our human nature will save us. We are too human to be trusted with atom bombs. We must rise to a new level, or we shall destroy one another.

So long as little boys have cap pistols and popguns they do no harm in shooting at one another, but with real guns those children can be dangerous. Today we are confronted with the horrible realization that the people in power on this earth are not spiritually mature enough to be safe with hydrogen bombs. The bomb itself is perfectly safe; it will not go off accidentally. But the men who can explode it

are not safe. As Einstein put it, living in this armed camp
has become intolerable. We must stop it. How?

One way would be to try a surprise attack and destroy
the enemy while he is still unable to retaliate. But there is no
sense in considering that possibility. The conscience of the
American people would not tolerate so monstrous a crime.
We are too Christian for that.

If we cannot tolerate this armed camp, and yet are too
decent to destroy the enemy and try to rule the world ourselves, then what is there left for us to try? Just one thing.
We can try to turn our enemies into friends, to change evil
men into good men, to remove the causes which produce
enemies, to have a world-wide religious revival.

Many will reply that this cannot be done. Maybe not.
But at least it can be *tried*. It *must* be tried, for a Christ-like
God wants it done this way.

I do not share the pessimism of many people. My work
has taken me all over the world, and I have had a chance to
see how miraculously whole nations can be changed from enemies to friends within one year when we go all-out to win
their friendship. I know, too, that we can make evil human
nature good, for I have seen that happen, too.

In his book, *Human Nature and Its Remaking*, Ernest
Hocking says that the gray matter in our brain is the easiest
stuff in the world to change. Indeed, every sense impression
from outside keeps changing it every second. He proves not
only that human nature can be changed, but that it *is being
changed* everywhere all over the world, all the time.

But we don't need a philosopher to prove this. Hitler
proved it when he changed the youth of Germany *in the
wrong direction!* Stalin proved it when he changed the entire viewpoint of the people of Russia *in the wrong direction*.

We could change the world *in the right direction* if we
would work as zealously for right as these men worked for

wrong! We know what the right direction is. It is the way of Jesus Christ. We could make the whole world right if we joined in an all-out crusade for the way of Christ.

But before we can change the world like that, we American Christians must first change ourselves. We are sixty per cent sham in our following of Jesus today. That is all too easy to prove. Christ told us, "Love your neighbor as yourself." He did that. If *we* did it, we could save the world. But we are counterfeit Christians. We do not love our competitors in business as we love ourselves. Or do we? Still less do we love the people of other countries as we love our own people. The very idea of doing that sounds unpatriotic—or like a violation of our Constitution! But until we do love our neighbor-nations as we love ourselves, we can neither win them as friends nor change their ways.

We must prove that love with unselfish deeds. Communism began because the masses of Russia were in poverty and the Communists promised to give them something better. Communism breeds today wherever people are hungry and dissatisfied. Who will deny that? About fifteen hundred million people, two thirds of the world, who are hungry and unhappy today hear the promises of the Communists, and they will go communist unless they are assured that we will help them out of their misery.

The answer to the promises of the Communist is clear; it is to go with a compassionate program of helping needy people to help themselves, and so prove that we are their friends. If we did enough of that we could make those fifteen hundred millions our firm friends. We could win even Russia and China back to our friendship. One of two things would happen. Their governments would change, or the people would overthrow them. The issue is very clear. Lift those fifteen hundred millions out of the pit of want or they will hate us and our system.

As we write, both the Democratic and Republican parties are promising the American people every good thing they can think of in order to win votes at the next election. It is the extreme of misfortune that every needy man, woman and child in the world can't share in that promise, for then they would be treated as *we* like to be treated! The countries of Asia cannot vote for our candidates, *but they will vote for America or for Russia*. We could lose Southern Asia at that ballot box, even if we placed hydrogen bombs in every port. Our own democratic system of elections will defeat us unless we prove to the Asiatics that we are their friends, and that we will help them out of their misery in the free, Christian, democratic way. *America is running for election in Asia*. Nobody contradicts that, and yet millions of Americans constantly work against the larger interests of the nation for their own selfish purposes. Nothing will stop their selfishness except the love of Christ. When His love acts in them they lose their selfishness and catch more of His compassion, just as did the engineer whom I decribed a few pages back.

This is why we need to return to Christ *now*. We do not have enough love for the hungry masses *unless we get it from Christ*. Compassion for the multitude was born on Christmas Day. There was mighty little compassion for the masses before Christ, and there has been mighty little of it since Christ that did not trace back to Him. When a life yields completely to Christ then compassion can channel through Him to needy men as it did through St. Francis, C. F. Andrews, Florence Nightingale, and Kagawa.

President Truman, in his 1949 inaugural address, proposed the "bold new program" to help the whole world help itself by sharing our technological knowledge. This he called "Point Four of his general program." Did Mr. Truman realize that, from the viewpoint of meeting human need, God had made him the spokesman for the greatest ethical advance in all history? The United Nations eagerly took up the idea, and today there are Point Four programs and United Nations programs for world help in nearly all the underdeveloped areas of the world. *Outside* America the world received the "bold new program" with unanimous approval. But *inside* the United States it has been fought by every form of selfish interest. Very few people oppose helping the world with our technical skills. The chief argument is: "Keep government out of it and let business do it for profit."

There are certain areas of this program which private enterprise should do and is doing. Westinghouse and Morrison Knutson, and Knappen-Tippets-Abbett-McCarthy, and other engineering firms are doing billions of dollars' worth of work for hydroelectric and power development all over the world. They are doing it better and cheaper than the government could do it. But several of the areas which are the most needy bring no profit, and private enterprise will not provide services for them on an adequate scale. For instance:

There is no money in teaching people to read and write.

There would be no profit in publishing cheap good literature.

There is no money in improving the health conditions.

There is no profit in showing farmers how to farm their land better.

There is no immediate profit in teaching people home industry.

There is no profit in teaching people how to raise their children.

These things must be done (1) by the government, or (2) by the United Nations, or (3) by philanthropy, or (4) by the church. The motive for doing them must be *compassion*.

This, then, is the question: How can we get enough Christian compassion to do these nonprofit types of service.

The Communists are telling the world: "America is doing this because she is in fear of Communism. The moment she stops being frightened she will stop helping you." Are the Communists telling the truth? Are we driven only by fear? Or can we rise to a spiritual level on which this new world service can be sustained as a long range program? This depends on how powerfully the motive of Christian love can take hold of us. We cannot, and will not, lift the world out of its dangerous desperation unless the Christ motive is strong enough to do it. That is why we had better pray for this revival! We had better pray for it to be a world revival, because America cannot, and should not, try to lift the world alone. It must become *world compassion*.

But we also need a revival of the religion of Jesus Christ within our own shores to save our democracy. The Communists believe that our system will destroy itself. They are wrong. If it collapses it will be because too many Americans placed self above their fellow men. Selfishness will destroy us, not democracy. Democracy is the finest type of government in the world. It is also the most demanding. When it really works, government is ruled by the majority. It is only as good as the majority make it. Democracy places very high demands on Mr. Average Man. It places a demand on his intelligence. But it places an even higher demand on his integrity and his public spirit. Where America's democracy fails today, it fails, not because of lack of intelligence, but because of lack of public spirit. This is not easy to say. The moment you say it you are hurting somebody. And that somebody may be reading this book.

Let me illustrate this with an extreme example: I have visited all the world's supposed "republics." Half of them are not republics at all, but military dictatorships. They cannot be republics until their people have more integrity. One of these countries has thirty thousand laws which nobody keeps! If people bribe the officials they will not get into trouble. If they refuse to bribe the officials they soon are ruined. There is always a law to catch them! Without integrity and public spirit, democracy rots!

When we in America place personal profit above our country we are hurting democracy. The rising prices all over the United States in the midst of plenty—we have so much abundance we don't know what to do with it!—is due to selfish desire for gain. The President has rightly said that profiteers are willing to jeopardize the nation for their own gain. We used to believe in the law of supply and demand, but producers have learned the trick of holding back or even destroying supplies so that there will be less supply than demand. This is so common that we call it legitimate.

People would not do that if they placed the welfare of their country above their own profit. We have inflation for no other reason than that so many of us are engaged in profiteering at the expense of the rest of us. For example, when the bread makers of America agreed to raise the price, the only reason they gave was that they feared the Government would freeze the price; so they raised it while they could— and *not* because they needed more money.

When, inspired by Moral Re-Armament, a public-spirited man in Canada named Cecil Morrison set out to keep down the price of bread by introducing economies and taking a small profit, his praises were sung throughout Canada and the United States as though he were doing something extraordinary and patriotic. You know and I know that that is the way every one of us *ought to be*. And that is the way only the minority *are*. This old way of selfishness could exist in past years. It jeopardizes our country and freedom now.

People will say, "What do you expect? Isn't this the American way of life? Rugged individualism! America is so strong that she can take it!" The answer is that she could take it before, but she can't risk it in this new age.

The soldiers who were captured in Korea and who, under pitiless brain washing and torture, "confessed" that America used germ warfare, are now being tried for betraying their country. Yet they did not endanger our country one ten thousandth as much as the profiteers who are sacrificing the people to gain selfish profit. Why, I ask, do we not demand that the standard for business shall be as high as the standard for soldiers?

This low level of selfishness is especially horrible to the boys coming back from Korea. One of these boys returning with only one arm said, "I was fighting over there so that you would not have to fight over here." One boy in the midst of fighting wrote back to the War Department, "I am willing and dependable and expendable. Say when and where." They were offering their lives for us *while we continued to sabotage one another*. We need enough real Christianity to lift us up to practice the Great Commandment in our own country, "Love thy neighbor as thyself." That is the level to which business has not yet come. The Rotary Club makes "Service before Self" its motto, and many business men are practicing that motto. But the average man is not. We need enough religion to get that golden rule practiced by the vast majority. When we reach that point our democracy will be strong enough to survive and to conquer the world.

Where there is no true religion there is no educated conscience. Where there is no conscience there can be no democracy. This is why Governor Martin of Pennsylvania was right when he said: "Gentlemen, the trouble with our country is not our laws. It is the lack of true religion. We have often said, 'Eternal vigilance is the price of freedom.'

But we should write that in another way. 'Eternal fanning of the flames of true religion is the price of freedom.'"

But what do we mean by "true" religion? It is not enough for it to be *"true."* It must have *power*. It must have the vitality to arouse a *vast world compassion*.

Edward Barrett advocates a "Crusade of all Faiths." He points out that the Golden Rule is to be found in all the six major religions. This is a happy discovery. But *all* rules and laws, including the Golden Rule, have one defect: they lack *vitality*. They are not alive.

St. Paul discovered this in his own experience. He saw that the Jewish law told people what was right, but it lacked the vital power to make people *want* to do right. He found that power only in the risen, living Christ. When Christ came to live in Paul, He drove Paul out across the world in unconquerable zeal to save other men. When He lives in any man He sets that man's heart aflame with compassion.

Compassion for the multitudes burned strongly in Christ. You seldom find it on the pages of history, except where it was started through Jesus Christ. The other great religions contain the Golden Rule, but that rule lacks the power to drive men to compassionate service.

You ask about Mahatma Gandhi. Was he not a Hindu? Yes, but his compassion was inspired by C. F. Andrews, the saintly missionary whose compassion came from Jesus Christ. Andrews was the greatest incarnation of the love of Jesus in our modern world. Now the followers of Gandhi in India are on fire with the compassion which came from Jesus, even though they do not call themselves Christians.

So if Barrett means that we are to ignore the living Jesus, out of deference for other religions, that kind of syncretism will not produce the thing most needed. All religions accept Jesus as a man who once lived and gave us the Golden Rule.

But a dead Jesus is not enough. The power of Jesus lies *in His presence here now as risen Lord.*

We can, and we must, work with people who do not believe this, but our hope must lie in those who have a far more profound experience of Him as the living Christ. Compassion will flow from the hearts of those who have Christ in their own lives.

A *New York Times* dispatch from Geneva says that United Nations technical aid is slowing down. The nations are not giving what they pledged. They lack the vital compassion of Jesus. The same thing is true in Foreign Missions. Only those who are filled with the compassion of the living Christ continue to give themselves or their money. When they lose the living Christ their gifts for foreign missions dry up.

I write with deep conviction about this because I have believed in Jesus *both ways.* Before 1930 I held what many people call "the university man's religion." I believed that Jesus was probably the best man who had ever lived. But that beautiful memory of Jesus lacked power. I was a failure in my spiritual life.

Then I had a personal experience of Christ in Mindanao, Philippine Islands, which left me sure that he not only *lives,* but lives in my heart. When He entered my heart, he brought to me a tender compassion for the multitudes which has been the driving power of my life ever since. The living Christ put it there.

The only hope of this evil, selfish world is for the living Christ to abide in enough of us to change the spiritual climate of the world. He alone is able to change greed to compassion, fear to faith, and hate to love.

But that is only half of the story. When He enters into us *we become a part of the way.* God's highway runs straight through us! We become *his* physical bodies. That was the meaning of Paul when he wrote in Ephesians 3:19,20 "I pray that you may be filled full of God." When His power works in us He is able to do far more than we dare to ask or even think.

Now I am sure that Christ came and must live in everybody.

II

BECOMING SONS OF GOD

WHEN A SPOILED CHILD FIGHTS AND SHRIEKS FOR SOME-
thing he desires, as though his life depended on securing
that thing, he does not understand that in a week or a year
that thing will mean nothing to him. All of us are like that.
We cling to the advantages of this moment because, like little children, we are shortsighted.

We need the long view. Indeed, we are not mature
Christians until our point of reference is in eternity. We need
to see the summit of the mountain we are climbing. When a
man gets a vision far up into eternity, as Paul did, then no
loss on this earth, however big, can shake his peace or his
faith. His religion will not depend on what he has here. He
will be undefeatable. St. Paul, looking into the teeth of
death, saw not death at all, but only real life: "For me to live
is Christ, but to die is to gain more of Christ."

Moreover, if we can look into eternity, we will never
hesitate to be unselfish. We will see that we never can give
anything away, that what we give away here may or may
not come back to us in *this* life, but it is sure to return to us
manyfold in a future life.

There are people who advocate a completely selfless life
which asks for nothing in this life or the next. I think that is
unnatural. Such selflessness kills one of our two greatest

25

driving instincts. Buddhism asks us to kill all desire. But Jesus does not ask us to desire *nothing*. He asked us to take the long view and to find our highest self-realization in eternity. "Great is your reward in heaven." Christ does not ask us to be selfless. He asks us to be *big* and to take a long view.

If we follow Jesus, then we will live a life of self-giving to the end of our earthly days, with no regret, no self-pity and no self-praise. We will not even call ourselves noble. We will just be wise and far-sighted. We will treat every other person with infinite reverence, for he is eternal. All these things above, below, around us decay. Even our granite monuments at last will wear out, or some irreverent person will destroy them. The mummies of Egypt are falling to pieces. But the soul of a man is eternal. We shall meet him again. We will be reverent, therefore, if we meet him now.

If God has His way in each of us, our future is so dazzling that the imagination reels to contemplate it. Paul saw this, and he cried, "Eye has not seen nor ear heard, nor has it ever entered into the heart of man what God is preparing for those who love him."

There are two chapters in the Bible which seem to me to hold the most stupendous visions in all the literature of mankind: they are the first chapter of Genesis and the eighth chapter of Romans. *LIFE* magazine for December 26, 1949, has some marvelous pictures photographed in the Vatican of Michelangelo's conception of God at the moment He was creating the universe. The eyes of God in that picture are indescribable. They are awe-inspiring, haunting. Seeming to comprehend God's purpose for His creation, Michelangelo painted in that titanic and terrible look of irresistible Will. The awful countenance reveals the mind of the Creator as He flung His universe into space.

When I was in the "know-it-all" stage common to heedless youth I discredited the first chapter of Genesis as a figment of the imagination. But science does not know as much now as it did at the beginning of the twentieth century. Today both the astronomer and the physicist have come back to the first chapter of Genesis, and they admit that it is the best description of creation that ever has been written. They say that between two and three billion years ago God gathered or created energy in one incomprehensibly dense ball, and then in an awful moment cried, "Let there be light!" And the ball exploded and flew out through interminable space to form the suns and the galaxies of suns and planets, so far apart now that it takes a light ray hundreds of millions of years to come from the most distant stars to our earth. Even the Hale 200-inch telescope on Mt. Palomar California, cannot see the farthest stars. The most distant stars are traveling fastest, just as would be the case if there had been a terrific explosion. The astronomers know where in space that ball of energy must have exploded when God first hurled his cosmic thunderbolt. And they can tell that it was three billion years ago from the distance which those pieces, which we call suns or stars, have traveled.

Therefore, if we interpret the "days" in the first chapter of Genesis as periods, then the scientists verify the Bible account. Many Christians do so interpret the "days," because the Bible says, "A thousand years to God are as a day."

One of the wholesome facts about the scientists of our age is that they are humble, not "know-it-all," as they were when Herbert Spencer started to write a complete explanation of the universe. And they stand in open-mouthed awe at the power and wisdom of the God who is behind the world we see.

But I think the eighth chapter of Romans is even greater than the first chapter of Genesis, because here Paul tells, for the first time in history, *why* God made the universe. Now we step out beyond science. Why did the Creator hurl those myriads of suns into space in that first superb hour when He created the universe? Paul says he knows. He says that God's purpose was to create sons of God, to beget us and to train us to grow at last into the full stature of His Son. And we know what that means because we have seen His Son Christ.

All that we see with a 200-inch telescope, Paul says, has that divine purpose. Is it a purpose just for this one little earth? No one can answer that question. No one can even dare to try. We do not know how many planets like ours there may be. That makes no difference. But what does make a difference is that we shall treat each other more reverently when we realize that three billion years of time and more than a billion light years of space measure God's incomprehensible effort to bring us forth.

We shall realize then that we are employing sons of God in our factories and on our farms. We shall stand aghast at the thought of measuring God's sons against so many productive "work hours." We shall appraise everything we undertake, not by what we can accumulate or gain from it, but by what it does to the souls of those who are working with us and for us. We shall some day consider it the most heinous of all sins to cramp or stultify the growth of a soul in the interest of selfish gain.

Now let us look straight into this dazzling, breath-taking conception of the universe and of what it was made for, and of what man is destined to become. Paul must have got this when he was caught up into the third heaven and heard things that mortal tongue cannot utter. He said, "The whole creation has been groaning in the pains of childbirth until now, and the creation waits with eager longing for the birth of the sons of God. When they appear, then the creation itself will be set free from decay." So this universe is a delivery-room for the sons of God! It is more than that; it is the kindergarten for the sons of God. We are born here, and here we get our first training for eternity.

This planet is our school; it is also a series of examinations. Day by day we are trained, and day by day we are tested to see how far we have advanced. "This," says Paul, "is the meaning of trouble." Trouble in our life here is like problems in mathematics to a student. The tests which help us grow are temptations, pains, disappointments, and struggles. These are our spiritual muscle-builders.

Robert Browning, who saw this, said, "Welcome each rebuff that turns life's smoothness rough." It is God testing us. Paul went through more of that testing than any other Christian in the Bible record. He was fought by the enemies of Christianity, and he was fought by those inside the Christian Church who thought that he was a heretic. Time after time, he was persecuted and almost killed. And always, when this suffering came to him, he had two consolations: first, it was a part of his education for eternity; and, second, his Lord had gone through it ahead of him and understood it all. Christ met abuse, misunderstanding, agony and death. When He was arrested in Gethsemane His disciples fled, but He went on to the cross. And it was years before they learned His secret and could die as He had died.

Robert Browning sings in *Bishop Blougram's Apology*:

When the fight begins within himself,
A man's worth something. God stoops o'er his head,
Satan looks up between his feet—both tug—
He's left, himself, i' the middle: the soul wakes
And grows. Prolong that battle through his life!

Again, Browning says,

Held, we fall to rise
Are baffled to fight better
Sleep to wake.

If we are on the way toward "that far-off divine event toward which the whole creation moves," we can judge how marvelous that end must be by the type of training which God gives us. I cannot understand why He subjects other people to the miseries which they suffer or allows them to suffer as they do, because I cannot see inside of them. The only person I can study from the inside is myself. I want to testify that, as I look back over my life, those periods which looked the hardest to me, those when I suffered the most, have turned out to be the periods in which I grew the most. And those periods in life which were easy and pleasant and free from struggle turn out now, as I look back, to be the periods of coasting, not of *rising*. For the soul, as for moun-tain climbers, *rising is work*. Life is easy only when we are on a level or going downhill.

"Well, then," I say to myself, to my soul, "stop grum-bling. God let this happen, and He is the perfect teacher."

One of the great values of athletic training is that it disciplines us to be good losers, never to grumble and never to lose patience.

Now the wise man learns to look on life as the athlete looks on a game. He may lose today and tomorrow, but he knows that he will not lose the war, even though he loses many a battle. He knows that all things, easy and difficult alike, are working together for ultimate good to those who love God. He doesn't rebel against God's arrangements to-day, against God's textbooks, or God's curriculum, or God's difficult problems, or His high goals. He is in training for the incomprehensibly wonderful life that lies ahead.

I suppose that this eternal life will not be the same for all of us. I don't believe that all this grooming and enduring hardships, this being buffeted about, is getting me ready to wear a white robe and to play a harp. If God intended us to play a harp through eternity I would rather spend my life here taking music lessons. Perhaps God is preparing the music lovers for that. We can infer what He is going to do with us in eternity from the training that we get here. I think He plans for many of us to continue in the conquests of seeming difficulties, in cosmic achievements of creation.

But did Paul's magnificent conception that we are becoming sons of God agree with that of Jesus? Yes, it did. In Matthew 5:44-45 Jesus said, "Be sons of your Father who is in heaven." How did He tell us to do it? He said, "If you have enemies, overcome their hate with love. If you have persecutors, overcome their persecution with prayer. If others do you harm, return it by doing good to them."

Then in Luke 20:35,36 He said, "Those who are worthy to attain the resurrection are sons of God and cannot die any more."

One of the most interesting statements of Jesus was made when His foes took up stones to kill Him because He said He was the Son of God. If we understood this statement of His, it would throw light on who we are and where we are going. They said to Him, "You are only a man, but you make yourself God."

And Jesus answered, "Is it not written in your law, 'I said you are gods?' If those to whom the word of God came are called gods, do you say, 'You are blaspheming' when I say I am the Son of God?"

What does this mean? It means that Jesus is what we are to *become*. He said the same thing in His prayer in John 17. "The glory which you gave me, I am giving to them. They shall be with me where I am; the love which you have for me will be in them, and I will be with them." I could quote many other passages that mean the same thing. Here is the key to the mystery of the universe, according to Jesus and according to Paul.

The world around us is God's best idea for helping us

grow into His sons. It isn't perfect because it needed to be imperfect so that we would have something to work on. Its imperfection makes it a *perfect* place as a gymnasium in which to develop our muscles and to become strong sons of God.

Sir James Jeans, the great astronomer, sees in the heavens the hand of a super-mathematician and a sublime architect, and most scientists agree with him. That is only another word for a "creator." The Creator is an architect. He first had the idea, and then He brought it into realization.

All of us, as sons of God are creators and bridge builders. We are God's co-creators. He is training us in this school of life by presenting us with an endless variety of problems, Many of them are just beyond our powers. In struggling to master them we grow. As we conquer one problem, another one more difficult confronts us, not to dismay us, but to challenge us.

A healthy body and a healthy mind look forward to an infinitely glorious succession of even more wonderful achievements. Walt Whitman expressed this in his sublime poem called *Passage to India,* which ends like this:

> O my brave soul,
> O farther, farther sail!
> O daring joy, but safe! Are they not all the seas of God?
> O farther, farther, farther sail!

Even more exciting than Walt Whitman's touring of the universe as an admirer is the conception of our helping God's never-ending creation of new universes—of sons working in blissful harmony with the Father and with one another.

One of the high qualities that this school we call earth must develop in us is *utter dependability.* It is the quality which cannot be tempted to falter or fear or sell out for any bribe. We are tried in a million ways to test whether God

can be sure—surer than sure—that, no matter how great
the responsibility He places on us, we shall still be faithful
to Him.

According to the Bible—and John Milton—God's chief
desire among angels as well as among men is to find the same
perfect loyalty and co-operation as he found in Christ. In
II Peter 2:4 we read that Satan and his fellow angels were
imprisoned in "pits of nether gloom" because they did not
obey. Milton's *Paradise Lost* amplifies this theme; the epic
says that God gave His angels powers so great that they
thought they could usurp God's throne. Satan and his le-
gions revolted against God but were overwhelmed and were
hurled into hell.

Now, in this last half of the twentieth century, God
seems to have taken another very long chance with us humans. He revealed to us one of the ultimate secrets of His
creation—the incredible power imprisoned in an atom. He
is letting us human beings know how to destroy ourselves
and our race and perhaps our planet. He is saying to us, "I
trust you with this. But you will destroy yourselves with it
unless you can treat one another with the reverence that
belongs to eternal sons of God, not like powers in a selfish
game, not like expendable cannon fodder." It seems as
though God were issuing an ultimatum to the human race:
"Rise to a new level, or perish by your own hand." Of course,
ultimately, God Himself cannot be harmed if we fail Him
and destroy ourselves. Yet if we fail God, it is God's failure,
too. It is His disappointment as well as ours. He must begin
all over again and develop a new human race, as He did in
the days of Noah.

There are deeper truths than we have been able to see
in this chapter. God's mind is infinitely beyond ours. I suppose that Paul had his finger on a truth when he said, "What
if it is necessary for evil to exist in order to bring out the

goodness of God, as a black background is necessary for a picture?" And I suppose some day, perhaps at the end of some eternity, every one of us will gasp as we behold the utter wisdom and goodness of God's total plan.

But in our day, knowing so little, like a fly on the edge of a great painting, we cannot begin to comprehend the total plan. All we can do is to trust. We have seen enough of God to know that He is good, and we can wait until we know it all. It is not necessary for us to know all about God. Our part is to be sure that we are *dependable*.

While we must try to understand God, we must never forget this: *God is not on trial*. Once a man visited the Louvre in Paris, which contains the world's greatest collection of art. As he came out he said to the guard, "Your pictures are no good. I am disappointed." The guard replied, "Sir, those pictures are not on trial; you are!" We must never forget that God is not on trial, but that we are. One thing we can understand about God is this: *God waits!* He waits from century to century until He finds men and women whose hearts are so open to Him and to their fellow men that His love can flow through them as it flowed through Jesus Christ. There is always a limitless reservoir of His love. But the world remains thirsty for love because too few of us are pipelines from heaven to the thirsty world.

We have been too much like Adam. We have gone against the will of God. And then we have hidden from Him. Alas, it is easy to hide from God—or to *think* we are hiding. All we need to do is to forget Him. God's voice is so still, so small, and the other voices around us are so loud. So you and I ignore God's voice. Especially in this noisy age our minds are like radios which let trivial messages from some near-by station drown out some great message from afar.

As we become wiser we shall realize the infinite importance of the infinitesimal. All of the achievements of science today are the result of paying more attention to the smallest detail. Gasoline could be harnessed only when cylinders could be ground down to a millionth of an inch. The camera and the motion picture are triumphs of infinite accuracy, and the radio and the television are even greater results of the mastery of even the most delicate light waves. Atomic energy and the atom bomb itself are results of understanding and mastering the smallest things in the universe.

Becoming dependable, grown-up sons of God is a matter of learning to give attention to the still small voice of God. His voice is more delicate and refined than the smallest physical thing in the universe. Hearing the whisper of the Spirit, as Jesus heard it every instant, and obeying every whisper that comes from the Father—this is the perfection for which the school of life must train us.

I close this chapter with one more thought. There was one step God had to take which was the most courageous thing, I think, He ever did. *He is bent on making us sons, not robots, not automatons, not work animals, and so He had to give us freedom to obey.* He seems to be saying to us: "I must allow you to try every way until you learn that all ways except my way are disaster. I must take this long chance with you, and it may be very long, indeed. I will let you wander through millenniums, if you want, but I will follow you to the end and in some future aeon I will have my prodigal son back home."

III

CHRIST OPENS THE WAY

BECOMING SONS OF GOD IS OUR GOAL. THIS MEANS THAT WE are to become like God's Son, Jesus Christ. Then our question becomes: "What is Christ like? How does He behave toward His Father, and toward His Father's work?"

The first thing we notice about Jesus is His everlasting obedience to the Father's will. The Gospel of John says 49 times in 49 different ways, words that mean simply that the Son can do nothing of himself, and that He does only what He sees the Father doing. "I have come down out of heaven not to do my will, but the will of him who sent me."

So to become perfectly Christlike means to become perfectly obedient to the will of God.

This is what Christ asks us to do. "If you keep my commandments, just as I keep my Father's commandments, you will abide in my love as I abide in his love. . . . You are my friends if you do what I command you."

Experience has taught us that such total obedience is impossible if we have to do it in our own strength. If that is the price of sonship we are defeated from the start. Much of the time our wills refuse even to want to be that submissive. If we force our wills to a reluctant obedience we shall be far below the obedience of Jesus. So, at first glance, there seems to be an impossible gulf fixed between us and Jesus.

But Jesus promises that His Holy Spirit will enter us and give us the will to do God's will. Then we will obey, not because duty is the "stern daughter of the Voice of God," but because there is nothing in the universe we want so much to do. When we love somebody enough, our supreme joy is to do what he wants done. So the Holy Spirit makes us love God so much that we yearn with one supreme desire to please Him. Such perfect love transforms every hard task and even death itself into joy.

Jesus' incredible, never-ending listening and saying, "Yes," made it possible for God to trust Him with literally everything. The Bible says that God has "put everything into His hands, everything in the universe," because He found that He could depend on Him so completely. It is not sacrilegious to say that Jesus earned the confidence of the Father by being trustworthy every moment, under every trial, in every detail. The Son and the Father have no disputes, because the Son never disagrees. The Son knows that the Father is always right. The Father never finds it necessary to persuade a reluctant Son.

We, too, are becoming sons of God, and we must learn this unflinching loyalty that never falters when a cross lies ahead. This is the first Christlike quality.

But even if we are willing to obey God every instant, as Jesus did, how are we to know God's will? Jesus knew it because He heard God speaking all the time. Can we hear God like that? Or must we always be as we now are? Must we be forever wondering what God's will is, but hearing no answer to our question? Millions of people are desperate to know what God wants them to do. Perhaps half the human race hesitates between two courses of action at this very hour.

That is the reason why *In His Steps or What Would Jesus Do?* by Charles Sheldon, sold nearly thirty million volumes; next to the Bible it is still the world's largest seller, because so many people hoped that in that book they would find the answer to the question: "How do I know what God wants?"

Is there a great gulf fixed between Jesus and us, so that He, coming down out of heaven, could know everything, while we, living on this earth, must be satisfied to know only a little? Is the song, "Teach me the patience of unanswered prayer," the best we can do?

You want a straight answer to that question. Here it is. I believe we often *do* get God's answer almost the instant we ask for it, *but we do not like God's answer,* and so we persist in asking, hoping that God will answer otherwise. I believe we should ask God for an answer; I also believe that when we get a reasonable thought or course of action, we should believe that God gave it to us, and act on it. We must accept it as an act of faith.

But you reply, "It is so easy to deceive yourself!" That is true. It is easy to think we are wholly open toward God, and our minds may be tricking us. It is the easiest thing in the world to mistake our own wishes for the call of God. How, then, can we know when it is God and when it is wishful thinking?

The answer is that we must spend more time listening to God. We forget to listen nine-tenths of the time. We suppose that if we listen for a few minutes God ought to be prompt and answer us then. I want to testify that in my life at least I can never accuse God of not answering my prayer, but it took *time!* If you have a wet shirt, and put it out in the sun to be dried and it isn't dried in two minutes, you know better than to be angry because it is not dry. It takes more time than that. And so does prayer.

If you want a college education, you can't walk through the college campus and then say you have "gone through college." It isn't done that way. We must be there when the knowledge is made available. The perfect student misses nothing.

Jesus was always listening for God. He was always there with His ear to the phone when God was ready to speak, so He never missed a word.

But all of us listen to God so seldom! We would blush to have anybody know how much we neglect God's voice.

Suppose you make up your mind to listen more constantly. Then you want a straight answer to the question *"How* shall I listen?"

Mrs. Sarah Schofield has a prayer group in her New York apartment. They pass around pencil and paper, and sit in silence. Presently, fingers are flying as they try to keep up with the flow of their ideas. Do the ideas come from heaven? As one listens to the reading of the papers after a half hour of silence, one feels that some members heard heaven speaking and some heard the spirit of this world speaking. Sitting in such a group is a powerful aid to concentrated attention. And where we are sufficiently attentive, heaven is always ready to speak.

But to the question: "How shall I listen? How shall I hear God's voice?" Jesus gave an answer so profound that hours of thought will not plumb it. Only years of experience will prove how true it is.

Jesus said, "He that is willing to do his will *shall know.*" The first condition of knowing is being willing to hear the truth. Many of us are afraid of what God will answer, and so we dismiss that still, small Voice because we do not want what we fear we will hear. As a matter of fact, we are often pretty sure that God will disagree with our own will.

Jesus' answer is, "If you want to do God's will, he will speak."

I have never met anyone who persisted lovingly in the quest of God's will who did not find it.

The second supreme quality in Jesus Christ, was that *He was perfect in love*. In what way was He perfect in love? I think, in the first place, that His love *reached out further* than ours. We love our family most, then our intimate friends, and then our school, then our club, and then our nation. The further from ourselves we go, the weaker becomes our love. But Christ's love reaches all the way around the world. In the second place, it is a warm love, always warm, no matter how far it reaches. It is like the sun. Compared to His bright sun, our love is like twinkling stars. His healing power was so much greater than ours because His love was so much greater than ours, and what we find impossible He found easy.

Jesus' love had a healing quality. It healed and cured instantly all that it touched. It turned disease into health and sin into saintliness.

His love was contagious. It flowed into others and then flowed out from others who came under His spell. Indeed, it was so contagious that you can see it in people's eyes and faces and hear it in their voices today, after two thousand years. People of every climate and of every tongue fall under His spell and catch that strange kind of love that He had. It was a compassionate love, which reached down to the depths.

It was not an easy-going affability. It was a mighty force. It wasn't a gentle breeze; it was a terrific, powerful wind. When He was around, one felt that love. The sick, the weak, the despairing felt His love pulling them, and rushed to Him as a piece of iron rushes to a magnet. Rulers and oppressors felt it and trembled with fear. It wasn't personal magnetism. It wasn't will power. It was pure, strong, resistless love.

The cross is the great symbol of the extent to which Christ will go in His love for us. "No man has greater love than this, that he lay down his life for his friends." But on the cross He went further than dying for His friends. "God showed his great love for us in that while we were yet sinners, Christ died for us." He did not die for good people; He died for people who did not deserve it and did not appreciate His death. His passion to help was so powerful that He died for us, not because we were lovable, but because we were hateful. Every angel in the universe would loathe such creatures as we were, so he died to change our hatefulness into lovableness. We were helplessly caught in sin. He helped us because we could not help ourselves. He died, not only for the sinners, but for His enemies. He died to save those who crucified Him. On the cross He could cry, "Father, forgive them, for they know not what they do."

This kind of love, so intense and so selfless, is what He depends on to save the world. There are three ways to treat enemies that we find advocated in the world today: First, *kill them!* Second, *get as far away from them as you can.* Third, *try to make them your friends.* But Jesus went beyond all three of these. He tried a fourth way. His plan was, "Let them kill you and keep on loving them. After you are dead they will realize how much you loved them and it will break their hearts and redeem them." He could have killed His enemies, but He let them kill Him.

Jesus expected that such love, set free in deeds of compassion and self-sacrifice, could save the world. I think that here we see behind the veil into the very heart of God. Here we catch, for a moment, the stupendous adventure on which God has started. He has let us try every other method under the sun of making a good world. At last we discover that love as selfless and as intense as the love of Jesus is our only hope of saving the world.

If Jesus loves like that, then we, as other sons of God, are to love like that.

We see, then, that to become like Jesus our present nature must be transformed by Him into an intense passion to help those in need. This is what He means when He says, "You, therefore, must be perfect as your heavenly Father is perfect" (Matt. 5:48).

In the third place, Jesus was perfect in *faith*. This is extremely difficult for an educated man to understand. Our scientific training insists upon testing everything, not in believing what we cannot prove. The Christian life takes the opposite view, emphasizing that we believe the best about God even when we cannot prove it.

Jesus had to fight a terrific battle for His faith. There had come to Him an inner conviction that He was the Son of God. He felt it, but He also pondered: "I am the only one who feels this way about Myself. Am I right?" He struggled 40 days in the wilderness with that question, and when He was very hungry the voice of Satan said, "If you are the Son of God, then turn that stone into bread and eat it. If . . ."

And again the voice of Satan said, "If you are the Son of God go and jump off the pinnacle and land among the people. If . . ."

Again the voice of Satan said: "If you are the Son of God, compromise and you can have the world." It would have been a short cut to world conquest. He could have done it. He had powers above any civil official or any military commander of His time. He *could* have overthrown Cæsar. Compromise would have been a good short cut. But it would have been the devil's victory over faith.

Our age and every age before us has been caught in the great doubt; we are in the midst of it now. Our nation is caught in it. We are saying, "Trust God and pile up your

hydrogen bombs." We trust love and hate at the same time.
We are compromisers. We can't trust love and we do not
trust God alone as Jesus did. We believe (more or less) in
Jesus, but we cannot be uncompromising in following love
as He followed it.

The temptation of Jesus to compromise was sharpened
by the fact that the Old Testament had prophesied two
kinds of messiahs. One was to suffer like the Messiah of
Isaiah 53; the other was to come like King David. David
trusted God and killed his enemies. Jesus trusted God and
refused to lift a finger to harm anybody. He suffered but He
never made others suffer.

To be a son of God involves faith in love and goodness.
To be like Jesus we, too, will have to refuse to compromise
with the idea of killing our enemies. We, too, must put our
faith wholly in love, the kind of love Christ had.

At once you and I begin to rebel against this idea. We
feel like the minister who said, "If a man came in to molest
my wife and children I would kill him. That is my duty.
And therefore," he said, "when enemies threaten my country,
they are threatening my wife and children, and I must kill
them."

That is what we all feel like saying. But it reveals a lack
of faith. It is not measuring up to the stature of sons of God.
All of us see that the devil leers at us in the atom bomb we
have begotten. We are seeing, to our dismay, that "they that
take up the sword will perish by the sword."

And yet mere refusal to fight with swords or guns is infinitely below the level of Christ's faith. Mere refusal to
fight would never save the world. I have been a pacifist all
my life, but a very uneasy one. To allow people to go and
get killed to protect me seems like a very cowardly thing. I
must earn my right to be a pacifist by fighting as hard as I
can all the greed and misery and hate that breed wars. I must

work for my country with the weapon of love as hard as others do by military means. I believe that we who put our faith in the love of Christ have not only got to *be willing* to fight with the love of Christ, and to sacrifice for it; I believe we must go out and *find a place* to sacrifice for it. We must not wait for need to come to us, but we must go out and find it!

C. F. Andrews is a great illustration in modern times of this kind of love. He went to any place in the world where men were suffering most, and there he suffered with them. Then he went to the powerful men who were oppressing them and pleaded with them to stop their oppression.

Andrews was in South Africa defending the Indians from oppression by his own people, the English, when he met Mahatma Gandhi; Gandhi was there as an attorney to protect the Indians. Gandhi's imagination and love were captured by this incredible kind of person who criticized nobody and loved everybody, this Englishman who came to the defense of the helpless and suffered with them. Gandhi learned that Andrews got this spirit from Jesus Christ. Gandhi began reading the New Testament with Andrews, and continued reading it all the rest of his life. This is where Gandhi got his idea of nonviolent and loving resistance. There is where he got his idea of compassion for the masses that led him to emancipate the Harijans and to break down castes. Gandhi said once, "If everybody in the world were like C. F. Andrews, I would be a Christian. But the Christian world is just the opposite of Christ." Gandhi, through the influence of Andrews, was the best incarnation of Jesus Christ that India has yet seen, though Gandhi rejected the word "Christian" because it had failed to be like Christ.

If one reads the Gospel accounts of Jesus until one thoroughly assimilates them, one gains an ever-growing realization of Christ's moral grandeur as compared to His own disciples. At last, one's admiration for Him becomes breath-taking. One falls on one's knees. "Love so amazing, so divine, demands my life, my love, my all." One trouble with us poor little humans is that we have to grow so much before we have eyes to see the greatness of Jesus! Even if one walks with Him for a lifetime, one realizes that out beyond is always a depth that one can not fathom. That is the reason why every attempt to make Him human has failed. The longer I read the accounts, the more the total picture of Him given in the Gospels fits in with His personality. He is the kind of Jesus who could feed five thousand people with five loaves and two fishes. He is the kind of person who could cure every disease wherever He met it. If we left out the miracles, He would be a man of very big words but small deeds. If He was what His disciples became convinced that He was—the Christ, the Son of the Living God—then we would expect what He did. We would be let down if He did not do these things.

The Gospel of John is to me the most precious book in the world. To me it reveals better than all the other books the intimate family relationship of Jesus and His Father. As we see that tender family tie we begin to realize what an incredible glory it will be to become a son of God. It will mean that we too are to join that household of the Father and the Son.

If we are becoming sons of God, then the most beautiful thing through all eternity will be to share the living, loving intimacy which the Father and the Son have. They live in perfect harmony, two wills as one, in a relationship that no words can describe: they have perfect faith in each other, perfect love for one another, such a oneness in their planning that Jesus could say, "I and the Father are one." Into that wonderful family He invites us. Jesus prays this wonderful prayer:

"Father, I desire that they also may be with me where I

am, and that as thou art in me, and I am in thee, that they may be one in us."

The religion of the Old Testament and all the other religions kept God at a distance. He was holy, and dangerous; the people trembled in His presence; they could not look into His face. "The fear of God is the beginning of wisdom." But when at last we achieve sonship and become sons of God, "we shall be like him"—intimate with the Father, and members of His family.

For that we are being prepared. We must become spiritually ready to respond to that perfection. We cannot spoil it by any whimsicalities, by being opinionated and stubborn and self-willed. To be in a perfect place, like the family of God, means that in love and responsiveness we, too, must be perfect. Otherwise we would spoil it. It is going to be a big family, and unless that family is harmonious and loving, free from criticism and from sharp, ungenerous, cutting remarks, heaven will cease to be heaven. So this long period of life that we are living on earth is mellowing us and sweetening us, and preparing us to be worthy so that we will not spoil heaven.

IV

GOD THE BRIDGE BUILDER

Dr. D. B. Steinman is one of the world's most famous bridge builders; he has received at least eleven honorary doctor's degrees for his services, and he makes his friends as fanatically devoted to bridge building as he is himself. His bridges are things of beauty. They are meant to be admired and loved as well as used.

Dr. Steinman has gone beyond his own field of bridging rivers and gulfs and canyons. Now he is trying to build bridges between people and nations. He sees that bridge-building is the chief unfinished task in human relations. How right he is!

Why is the brain the most marvelous machine in the universe? Because it has such a great, complex system of bridges—interconnections from one cell to another that can store up and transmit and transform and reorganize thoughts. I think no one has yet calculated how many thousand miles of such connections there are in one man.

Around the world our new miracle inventions—radio, television, telephone, motion pictures, airplanes, newspapers —are building fantastic bridges between one country and another. No one sees this more vividly than the radio and television and visual education pioneers. A leader in visual education said: "The big problem for God and for man is communication. It is a matter of getting ideas from where they are to where they are needed. God has the ideas; men need them." And today God is at work night and day weaving the intricate connections necessary for a "world mind."

The longer you think about that, the more certain it becomes. At last you see that bridges of one kind or another are necessary for every step in the long road of progress. The way is blocked without them. It is true that bridges are not *everything,* but they are a vital part of everything. Indeed, they are so much a part of everything that not even an atom can exist without bridges to hold its parts together. And that is not an exaggeration!

Name anything in the world. Some people have it, while others need it.

Teacher—pupil: the teacher knows, the pupil needs the knowledge. A thought needs a bridge to a hand, then to paper, then to a press, then to a book agent, then to a reader . . .

Or take iron ore. It is in the ground. How many stages it passes through before it ends in a locomotive!

Take a fish. It is in the sea. How many hands touch it before part of it ends in your mouth!

Not a single step was taken in God's vast eons of creation without endless bridge-building from God's infinite resources to space's infinite emptiness.

There are bridges between *wishes* and *fulfillments.* To us in this world, life seems to be a ceaseless rhythm of wishes and fulfillments. Wish long enough and, lo, it is done! Plato was the first great thinker to see this in his philosophy of "architectonic ideas." These ideas are first in the mind of God the Architect, and *then* they come into being.

God puts His ideas into our minds, and our ideas create telephones, radios, airplanes, the United Nations! Here is one respect in which we are truly "sons of God" even now. I think our chief joy in all eternity will be to be co-creators with God. And half of this creation will be a matter of bridge-building.

Lecomte du Noüy, in his tremendous *Human Destiny*, has accumulated evidence from modern biology that there is a master mind hidden deep within every living thing. The single cell, whether of a tree or a butterfly or a bird, starts life as an embryo. No life could ever unfold, the biologist now sees clearly, without a master mind inside developing the various parts and breathing life into them.

This master mind not only works *within* every living thing, it works *among* them, keeping all living things in perfect balance with all others. It builds bridges between all living things.

It was not until this century that scientists discovered this amazing balance of bridges throughout the universe, because we little men have looked at everything from our own short-sighted viewpoint. We knew that the bee needed the flower, because we wanted the honey, but it was a long while before we realized that the flower needed the bee before it can produce other flowers. But today the scientist sees a vast exquisitely balanced world at work in every clod of soil. Now he realizes that the fish worms are boring air holes and the tireless bacteria are all working together to make the soil digestible for the plant. God is there working before man comes with his plow and his seed.

God has His finger in the unfolding of not only every tiny cell but of every atom and every electron. What a finger it must be!

It makes one dizzy to think of this capacity of God to handle everything, everywhere, *every* minute. The more we know about this bewildering universe, the more amazed we become at God.

> These things are too wonderful for me.
> They are past finding out.

When Einstein, the most prodigious mind of our age, discovered that all material phenomena can be compressed into a single formula, God must have smiled, because that is the formula He started with on the first day of creation!

God has been at work building bridges all down through the aeons, and every great advance, at least what seems great to us, is great because new bridges have been built. We see that in our own generation. The human race was split up into a large number of human tribes with a different language behind each hill. And then bridges began to be built. Writing was one of them. Reading and writing have enabled people to communicate over the hills and across the oceans.

Before our very eyes God is tying the human race together. He is doing it with these miraculous modern inventions—the steamship and the railroad, the telegraph and the telephone, the ocean cable, the automobile, the airplane, the motion picture, radio, television: God is using these to create a *nervous system* and *blood stream* for the One World which is coming in the twenty-first century. The whole human race is becoming one organism. I do not mean the United Nations. A world *organism* is not to be confused with any world *organization* or government. Nevertheless, the United Nations is an outward manifestation of this growing organism and can be its servant, and, to some extent, its brain.

And now with this vast network of world bridges and this new unity it has become possible in our day to reach the whole world for Christ. It has never been possible before. When Jesus commanded His disciples, "Go ye into all the world and preach the gospel," it could not be done. As a matter of fact, the people in the Roman Empire did not *know* where the *rest* of the world was. There was no way for them to reach South Africa, or North or South America or the Far

East or the Islands of the Pacific. They did not even know the Western Hemisphere existed. Marco Polo, and later the Portuguese, and after them the explorers of Europe, pushed farther and farther, building new bridges across the world. But they were narrow bridges and meager in number.

Even as late as the last century, many a missionary who went to India or to South Africa or to South America would be a year on the way. It depended on the wind. Missionaries went planning to stay the rest of their lives. But with our modern steamships and airplanes it is possible for us to reach to the ends of the world quickly. Now we can "go and preach the gospel to every creature." We can go in person, if we wish, with this vast system of airplanes that has been built around the world, or our voice can span the seas with the radio—that astonishing system of world nerves—in a second of time. This new intricate network of bridges through the sky has almost abolished space, and the radio has all but abolished time. Now people can hear news of an event almost the instant it happens, no matter where they are!

Paul was exultant in Ephesus because, to use his words, "a great door effectual has been opened and there are many adversaries." *One city* filled Paul with joy. In our day the doors to *six continents* have been flung open and they swing wider every day!

Look at the incredible expansion of education. This is another of God's bridges. In the past, education was intended for a very small percentage of the people—for the aristocracy, for royalty, for the rich. Before the Reformation in northern Europe took place, it was customary in Europe, as in all parts of the world, for only one-half of one per cent of the people to have an education, while the rest were totally illiterate.

But Luther and the other leaders of the Reformation began to educate the masses. They said: "All men must be able to read the Word of God for themselves, for the Word is their final authority." And because they wanted people to be able to read the Bible they invented printing presses and began the movement which has eventually grown into our system of universal education for children.

In the last few years the world has interpreted "universal education" to include adults as well as children. In our own generation, especially in the past *ten years,* a worldwide titanic effort is getting under way which aims to teach a billion illiterates to read.

Governments as well as missions are engaged in this educational program. Many of them call illiteracy "Enemy Number One" to their program. Courses of study that are easy enough for "each one to teach one" are sweeping around the world. The World Literacy Committee has been invited to help fifty-six governments prepare their texts. Thus bridges of reading are being built into the minds of all the people in the world. Henceforth newspapers and magazines and books will disseminate new ideas among them in the same stupendous volume they disseminate among us now.

So this bridge-building is like all bridge-building that ever has been. Whether the bridges are good or bad depends on who and what goes over them. The bridges Xerxes built over the Bosporus to invade Greece, brought the Greeks disaster. During the two World Wars thousands of bridges were destroyed to prevent the enemy from passing over them. When the world's new nervous system is used by demagogues to pour hate and evil and venom into the world, as is happening now, the bridges are doing harm.

De Noüy says, "The conflict between intelligence and moral values is now a matter of life and death. Intelligence alone, when not subjected to moral values, leads to monstrosities." The new world's nervous system can destroy itself. But I, for one, do not believe it will. For I believe that God has been behind it all. I believe that today's evil is already arousing us to work harder to give the world what we believe it needs. The threat of Communism is stirring up the Christian world to awaken and help the rest of the world.

For the first time in history we *can* evangelize the world *if we want to.* And I believe that God is using threats of evil to make us want to! He built the bridges and now He is pushing us over them.

Here is a challenge to us to be bigger than we are. Some of us are overstimulated by this challenge. We are driven almost to hysteria by the realization that we are in a world that is so much bigger than we are, and that it challenges us to stretch our little minds. To us God is saying, "You must be big enough for this new age!"

The Church must crack its old shell, come out of that shell and grow, grow toward the fulness of the stature of Christ. A new John Wesley could do for the world today as much as, perhaps more than, John Wesley did for seventeenth-century England. He would not need to ride from village to village on horseback; he could fly his own plane. *If* we had a modern Wesley, we Christians would stop trusting our atom and hydrogen bombs to protect us from the Communists. We would start forth on a campaign of helpfulness to win the war for men's minds and hearts. We shall have to come to it, for the outcome of such a campaign will decide the world's fate. L. P. Jacks, in a book called *The Living Universe,* says this perfectly: "Because our minds and souls are so barren is the reason why we little people have always been leaning on material forces, on guns and power." If we had a more spiritual imagination, we would lean on the spirit. We would know that "soul force" is the greatest force in the world, as Mahatma Gandhi so abundantly proved.

God has built countless bridges to men's minds, but He has placed one limitation on Himself: He does not cross the last drawbridge into our minds until we invite Him. It is a drawbridge which we open and close from within the castle of our souls. Don't ask me why; I don't know. I suppose it is because He wants His sons to have free wills. Whatever the reason, God's final problem in bridge-building is to get past the portal of our own minds.

The statement of the risen Christ in Revelation, "Behold, I stand at the door and knock; if any man hear my voice and open the door, I will come in to him," is one of the strangest paradoxes in the universe. God made us, but He fashioned us so that He could enter our hearts *only* when we invite Him. We are invited to be sons, but we make the decision ourselves whether to be in God's family or not. We are free. God will wait, if He has to wait, a year, a decade, a century, or a thousand years. Why it is that way I do not know; but it *is* that way, as we know from our own experience.

In fact, there are *two* drawbridges in the castle of our soul, and the man within has control of both. One opens *up* toward God, and the other opens *out* toward our fellow men. If we open both our drawbridges we become God's *highway*.

This is what Luke calls John the Baptist: "The voice of one crying in the wilderness." Isaiah had prophesied:

> Make ready the way of the Lord;
> Make straight through the desert a highway for our God.
> Fill up every valley and lay low every mountain.
> Make every crooked road straight;
> Make every rough place smooth,
> Because all mankind is about to see the salvation of God.
> Luke 3:4-6.

John the Baptist was himself that "highway for our God." He was open at both ends. That was why he had power.

I saw this truth illustrated in Liberia. The social director of the Firestone plantation took me to see their great hydroelectric plant which runs their mill and supplies their light. I had never seen the inside of a hydroelectric plant before. There was a huge pipe, and four great turbine wheels. The water was open above them, but they were standing still. I said, "Why don't these turbines run?" He said, "Because the pipe is closed down at the outlet. If that were open, the water could flow through. The turbines can't run unless both the inlet and the outlet are open."

I said to this man, "That is the way our lives are. The pipe must be open up toward God and open down toward man. And then currents flow through and the wheels go round and we work with the power of God."

He said, "I never thought of that. I wonder where *my* pipe line is closed."

Many people who have opened themselves toward God have had a marvelous experience for a few minutes or a few hours, but because the pipe was closed at the bottom the spirit's flow came to a stop, and they wondered what was the matter. That has been the experience of many Christian people ever since Christ came. They have opened, they have received a great blessing, and then their Christian life has come to a standstill, and they wondered why! Their little bucket could hold only a small amount, and it was soon full. The infinite resources of heaven were awaiting them; all they had to do was to open the gate at the bottom—to kick the bottom out of their buckets—and to let God flow through. It doesn't matter how big heaven is; it matters how big our pipe is and whether it is open. The bottleneck is never God; it is always ourselves.

In one respect, however, we are different from a pipe. A pipe cannot decide how big it will be, and we can. We can grow. We are small pipes at first, but if we keep open all the time the total flow for a day and a month will be great and, as the flow continues, we will become bigger pipes.

How shall we keep open toward people? There are two ways. The first is by *prayer*. That prayer of intercession connects God and other people; it is one of the purest forms of service, the mightiest single power on earth. When we pray for others we open the pipeline at both ends, and God flows through to bless those for whom we pray.

The second great outlet to people is by deeds of *kindness*. It may be through *talking* to people. It may be through *feeding* them. It may be through *healing* them. Jesus spent His life in prayer for others, and in loving deeds. Any man who spends his life that way can forget all about himself, for he will be the most blest of all. The spirit pouring through him will make his soul sing, and everybody will see the glory shining through. The glory and the power are not his own. He is only the pipe line through whom the infinite power of God pours down to meet the infinite need of humanity.

We become channels like that simply by being willing and unselfish. But the moment we desire to keep any of the power for ourselves we cease to flow. If we strut and say, "Look at me," as the spirit passes through, that "me" obstructs the passage. The Spirit of God doesn't flow until the "me" is washed out and only the pipe line is left. That is the meaning of the paradoxical saying of Jesus, "Whosoever would save his life shall lose it: and whosoever shall lose his life for my sake shall find it."

Stop being a terminus and become a bridge! Stop being a bucket and become a pipe! That is the secret of receiving the power of God.

V

WHAT IS BLOCKING OUR CHANNEL?

ONE OF MY FRIENDS WROTE OUT THIS CONVERSATION, WHICH
he had with one of his acquaintances:

"What's the matter today?"

"How do you know anything's the matter?"

"Shows all over your face."

"I was trying to smile."

"It had a sickly look. Looked like something was blocking you."

"That's exactly it. I'm blocked."

"Which direction—up or out or inside?"

"It's resentment, deep resentment that I can't shake
off."

"By the way, I notice you're limping. What makes
that?"

"Arthritis. Do you think that is making me peevish?"

"No, but the arthritis is caused by your resentment. Indeed, arthritis is only another name for a sore mind. So are
stomach ulcers."

"Good heavens, man, I've got one of those, too!"

"God *is* good! He has brought your resentment to the
surface where you can get at it. God never can do anything
for a man until the man knows something is the matter
with him."

"Well, none of the treatments for my arthritis has done any good."

"Get rid of the cause, and you won't need any treatments."

"I've tried that, but you can't stop hating just by will power. The harder I try the deeper it goes."

"That is exactly right; it sinks deeper and does more harm. Stop trying and let Christ have it. Try to walk and talk with Christ until you love Him and trust Him. Let Him turn your bitter thoughts sweet."

"Christ has been dead two thousand years."

"You are wrong about that. He is alive. Millions of people every year have had sick minds like yours, and Christ has taken out their hate and their disease. He does more of that in this country today than He did in Palestine. Give Him a chance. He isn't dead. But *you* will be dead if you don't let Him help you. This poison you have in your mind is deadly."

"I've tried praying; nothing happens."

"How did you pray?"

"I asked the Lord to make my wife reasonable, so I could get this out of my system. I've prayed that a dozen times. Nothing happened."

"Do you feel any resentment toward God?"

"I might. At least He has disappointed me."

At every turn one finds defeated people like that. One man's face reveals a sour soul; another man's grumble reveals disappointment and cynicism.

For such people the first great question is, "What is blocking you?" They are like drain pipes that get clogged and have to be cleaned out every few weeks.

On the deserts of North Africa and Southwest Asia I have seen many a dead sea, with salt so thick that you could float on it, and so bitter that nobody dare taste it or get it in his eyes. Streams flow into those seas, but none go out. That is why they are bitter. On these deserts one will also see a great many dried-up lakes. These are totally dry because no water runs into them.

Every defeated person in the world is either like those salt lakes or else like those dried-up rivers. When he has no *outlet* in human kindness he is bitter. When he has no *inlet* from God he is dried up as well as bitter. When this happens it is not only the man's loss; it is God's loss, too. For God must channel His love to the world through hearts that are open toward Him and open toward other people.

Few people realize how hard God is trying to reach them. They suppose that they are reaching for a God who is eluding them. They are wrong. It is never God who shuts us out. The block is always somewhere inside ourselves.

How do we recognize a block and how do we break it? At the Camp Farthest Out at Lake Winnipesaukee we were seeking the answer to that question. Two hundred persons made voluntary statements about the things that had caused blockages in their lives before they came there. They had experienced marvelous releases and they longed to tell the world how it had happened. Nearly all of these two hundred had had their blocks removed while they were at the camp, and as they wrote their testimonies they were looking back at their recent past. They were judging from the inside what had been the matter with them.

This is valuable first-hand evidence. If a man were still blocked he would not know what was the matter with him nor how to get rid of it. But those who have found their blockages and have broken them can speak with real authority to the rest of us.

The people who wrote these answers are well above the average in intelligence and refinement. Many of them are highly educated people, and know the meaning of psychiatry. They had one other advantage. This was that they were writing under the inspiration of a glorious spiritual experience.

These conclusions do not come from any one man's experience. They represent the experience of two hundred people, with a wide variety of temperaments and problems. They gave seven hundred reasons for blockages, and I have organized these into different groups. Here they are:

Group 1. 186 persons said that *self-centeredness* had blocked them. Of these, according to their own confessions,

78 were selfish.

38 were proud.

48 were touchy.

10 did not love other people.

8 were stubborn.

4 were too independent.

Group 2. 181 persons said they were blocked by *feeling defeated*. Of these

76 said they had a sense of being inferior.

28 said they were nervous from fear of failure.

27 said they felt left out and were lonesome.

15 said their ambitions had been frustrated.

12 said they were plunged in despair.

23 said they were frustrated by difficulties which they could not surmount.

Group 3. 135 persons said they were *full of resentments*. Of these

31 disliked or hated people.

31 were jealous.

30 said they were too critical of others.

28 blamed their relatives and disliked them.

15 blamed people who were not their relatives.

Group 4. 119 persons said they were blocked because *they were not in contact with God.* Of these

> 55 said that "something" had broken their relationship with God and they couldn't get it back.
>
> 38 said sin had shut them from God. They knew God disapproved, but they couldn't give up the sin.
>
> 26 said they had neglected God.

Group 5. The big surprise was the small number of those who blamed *physical illness* for their blockage. There were only 24.

> 20 of them said they had been sick.
>
> 4 of them said they had a tired feeling.

The smallness of this group contradicts the impression that most of us have. If you and I were asked what blocked people, would we not be inclined to say that half of it was due to sickness? Yet not one-thirtieth of these people who had been released and looked back gave that reason.

The second surprise is that only 33 blamed other people for their blockages. And even those blamed their own resentment rather than the actions of others.

I was surprised also at the small number of those who said that they were blocked by their own sins. There were only 38 of these. They meant sins of the body.

When, however, you think of "sin" in the larger sense of the word, like the sins of hate and selfishness and separation from God, then the number shoots up. There were 402 who blamed such sinful states of mind as resentment, hate, or selfishness for their blockage.

Group 6. One is also struck by the fact that 251 persons attributed their blockage to fear and a "lack of faith" and a "sense of defeat." When we added resentment to fear (both morbid states of mind) we found that 9/10 of the causes of blockages are morbid states of mind.

Jesus did not call this "morbid." He called it "sinful." No wonder: Jesus, with His deep psychological insight, immediately pushed sin back beyond the deeds of the body into the mind and the heart. "Outward sins," He said, "are symptoms of a sin of the soul." All the 200 testimonies corroborated Jesus' statement.

It is remarkable that these people made these confessions. I do not think they would have confessed anything at all if we had requested it *before* they were released. People who are selfish or stubborn, touchy, proud, critical and jealous, do not admit even to themselves that they are in the wrong. And that is what is the matter with them. They cannot find the blockage because they refuse to look for it in themselves. They always blame someone else—never themselves. In fact, many people consider holding a grudge and getting revenge a sign of noble character. That was the ethical standard in the days of dueling. In the olden days knights in armor would go forth to avenge their insults; that was the highest level of their ethical life. Probably all of us remember our adolescent years when revenge seemed to be a sign of a strong character. It was weak not to take your own part. It was right not to let your adversary get the better of you. You remember how you dignified selfishness by calling it "ambition," and how you excused touchiness by calling it defense of honor. Criticism of others seemed to you to be a sign of your own keen intelligence. When you disliked people you thought it proved your "high standards of discrimination." If you were jealous of someone else you said that he was "greatly overrated." You were obsessed with proving that you were always right and other people always wrong. This is how these people felt before they got their release at the Camp Farthest Out at Winnipesaukee. Christ taught them to seek the trouble first inside themselves—and there they found it. And nine times out of ten it was a form of selfishness.

The incredible meanness of human nature is more apparent if one travels much in crowded trains or busses, or goes into crowded restaurants. Here we have in a mild form the same spirit that runs wild in a boat about to sink, when everybody struggles to save himself. When people are traveling they treat one another, as a rule, as strangers and aliens. This morning, for example, in Northern Rhodesia, two men were put in the compartment with us. One of them said, "Let us sit down." They took the seat by the window and stayed by the window until we found another empty room near by. Then they lost all their interest in the seats by the window and went up to the lounge to get a drink. If we had not found the other room, those men would have lost their drink just in order to hold fast to those seats by the window!

One sees this pettiness in treatment of strangers in every country and almost every day, and he keeps asking himself, "How can God take us ugly little people into heaven without spoiling heaven?" The same thing occurs in airplane travel. People crowd in to get the best seats. This has become so bad that in many countries they have to be given seat numbers. The same thing happens in subways and in busses. Who hasn't seen it?

Selfishness has a hundred faces, and it is the father of all sins. It is the deepest rooted sin, and the hardest for one to admit, and the hardest for him to eradicate. Removing it is a major operation.

What does selfishness do to our channels? It blocks them completely. God cannot use a man to help others when the man grabs all the best for himself. Selfishness not only blocks the selfish man; it has been blocking Jesus Christ Himself all down through the centuries. Two of the greatest leaders since the days of Jesus were Mohammed and Mahatma Gandhi. Both were unqualified in their appreciation of the grandeur of Jesus. But both repudiated us as Christ's followers because we are frauds in that we profess His love but practice selfish greed. So there is more truth than fiction in the statement: "The greatest hindrance to the spread of Christianity has been the selfish hypocrisy of Christians."

It is a very subtle blockage. Often nobody can see that choice but God. Many a minister preaching in a lovely church at a high salary knows in his heart that he selfishly sought that comfortable position instead of some difficult place in a slum or a foreign land where he would have to suffer to succeed. Deep in his soul he is aware that God sees his selfishness, even though nobody else suspects it. His conscience often blocks the power of God's Spirit.

Those high, stark, uncompromising demands of Christ that His followers shall *crucify selfishness* are not much taught today, and they are much less practiced.

But we who wish to be God's channels to the world must fiercely renounce the selfishness of the world.

But what will the world do to us if we do not watch out for our interests? It may rob us. It may crucify us. How can we prevent this? We can't prevent it. But we *can* suffer the loss—Paul did! We *can* die—Christ did! This much is sure: we can't be channels if we are blocked by self. We must make a choice. It can't be both.

There is another blockage for a great many people in our headlong age: they are too hurried. They allow this world to drive them to death. Their prayers must be prayed hurriedly. Their devotional books have to be one short page a day, so that they can pray and get it over with in one minute flat. What can we do about it? John R. Mott, our revered veteran religious statesman, tells us what he did about it. He

said, "My life has been so busy that I could not have carried it without two or three hours spent with God before
anybody else was up in the morning."

Nearly all of us can chop off one or two hours of
sleep early in the morning, if that is the only part of the day
that can be spared. In these days of electric lights and warm
houses nobody can find an alibi for failing to do that. Cul-
tivating the intimate friendship of God or of Jesus Christ is
a slow process—like the development of seeds into plants
and trees and fruit.

Today our mental hospitals are overflowing. Half of all
hospital cases are mental. There was less insanity in the
days of Jesus, and fewer nervous collapses. The reason is
plain. We are overstimulated. We are like the seeds which
fell among weeds. The cares of this world and the prejudices
and resentments and hurryings are not only choking out the
Word of God, but also pulling us to pieces and slamming
shut the doors of heaven.

If these two hundred witnesses at Winnipesaukee wrote
the truth, then nine times out of ten a man finds the cause
of his blockage in *himself*. This is very important evidence. If the blockage is inside, then that is where it must
be broken. Jesus said exactly that. He said, "Nothing outside
a man can injure him, but only what comes from within."
People who complain that they need better surroundings,
grumble at their neighbors, deplore the climate, cry because
they are poor or are discontented with their job, do not get
what they ask for, but succeed only in making themselves
more miserable. They make other people miserable, too.
They never win friends with their complaints. Even if
their condition were perfect, would they be happier? Most
of them would not be.

But if, on the other hand, they can win the battle with
self-centeredness in their own hearts, they will soon find the

outside world bending to adjust itself to their changed inside. Shakespeare's line, "The world is a mirror," is a far deeper truth than we realize. As Wordsworth says, "We half perceive and half create our world." Light enters our eyes from the world, and all the rest of it we imagine or construct inside the mind. It was said of Rufus Moseley (called by E. Stanley Jones "the greatest living saint") that he never found evil anywhere he went, because the moment he arrived the evil disappeared. On the other hand, many people see evil where none exists. The world tends to make itself over after each man's pattern, whether he be good or bad.

It is a mistake to complain about our job. "As soon as we are ready for a better job, that job is ready for us." If this is true, then when we complain we are asking for a change for which we are not yet ready.

Even in a bed of sickness one can believe that God is doing something for him which required that experience. Gil Sonastine of Columbus, Ohio, has been lying in bed with arthritis for thirty years, every day in pain, and so blind that he cannot see anybody. I asked him if he wanted to be well.

He replied, "Yes—and yet, do I? This experience has given me a knowledge nobody could possibly have without it."

I felt, as I looked at him, that I understood the words of Jesus when He said, "The man was born blind that the works of God might be manifested in him." At least, Sonastine taught me the lesson that a man on a bed of pain, utterly blind, unable to move, can have a wonderful experience of Jesus Christ. It isn't the outward condition that makes a difference. It is the soul within.

Two hundred fifty-one times, these folks at Winnipesaukee gave *fear* as the cause of blockage from God. Some said they were afraid God would ask too much of them! They were afraid that God might carry them to some cross and ask them to give up the things they most wanted. One camper said, "I shut myself off from God except for a little peephole on Sunday morning when the minister opened the window cautiously to heaven. I wrote vigorous letters objecting to the minister if he disturbed the congregation too much."

When people are afraid to give up their own wills to let God have His will, God has one final expedient. He capsizes their boat! Then they pray. When we wonder why God is allowing disaster to happen to people it may be God's last best answer to their unwillingness to give up their little wills in the interests of His bigger will. Every misfortune is good fortune if it drives us back to God.

While some of us are afraid to open toward *God*, a great many others of us are afraid to open toward other *people*. We are afraid people will hurt us or take advantage of us, or else take too much of our time. We are afraid they will abuse our friendship. So we peek through the door at new friends for a long time before we open it wide enough for them to come into our hearts.

Seventy-three campers said they had been blocked by a *habit of complaining* about everything in the world, including the weather. At the same time, a large number of people said they had been released from complaining about the weather because they realized that God makes the weather.

After their release, they could see God's hand at work, grinding away imperfections. Life is God's grindstone and His sandpaper; it smooths the rough diamonds of our souls. For we are diamonds in the rough. We complain when the polishing hurts. We want God to let us alone, but He loves us too much for that. He keeps on shaping and polishing us for some very high purpose. Much of that shaping is painless, but some of it involves pain. Is the pain a punishment for our sins? Some of it is, I suppose, but certainly not all of it. Jesus suffered on the cross, though He never sinned. And the book of Hebrews says that even Jesus had to be "made perfect through suffering." There is a kind of perfection that is far beyond sinlessness. It is the perfection of understanding compassion.

Notice that the two chief blockages to God which we have studied in people are at exactly opposite extremes. One is the fault of *too much* self-assertion, and the other of *not enough*. One is frustrated self-assertion, so evident when people want what they have not been able to attain. The other is a paralyzing sense of inferiority—so evident when people are afraid to *try!* The first tries too hard; the second doesn't try at all.

Under this second blockage—sense of inferiority—our Camp Farthest Out confessors gave a long sad list of fears. Here are some of them: Cowardice, worry, "fear of the future and of failure," "fear of criticism," "fear of pain," "fear of death," "fear of illness," "fear of making mistakes," "fear of being seen by people," "fear of what others might think of our appearance."

The world seems to be full of people who tried life for a while and lost and gave up the struggle. Here is how the Camp Farthest Out group labeled or described their sensations: the sense of defeat, intellectual difficulties, doubts, despair of financial reverses, depressions, pessimism, nervous exhaustion, overwork, self-pity, the sense of being pushed and hurried, intense loneliness, loss of self-respect, sense of being useless, stammering, sense of weakness, can't succeed at anything, in debt, a lack of fixed purpose, feeling like a hypocrite. "I just can't." "I am blocked by negative thoughts. I see the dark side of everything." "I couldn't find out what blocked me. I lay awake at night." "I can't tear away from my past."

This long sad list leaves us with a sickening insight into the hopeless half of the world. If these rare souls at Camp Farthest Out had so many skeletons in their closets, the fears and defeats of the average human being must be tragic beyond words!

We are called to enter God's family as sons. A total transformation must take place in our nature before we can join that family. How could it be a loving family if everyone were pushing the other aside, taking any advantage to get ahead, or backbiting, or feeling resentment? In the light of God's purpose to make us into sons, the sins that we condemn the hardest are far less obnoxious to the Kingdom of heaven than this ultimate sin of selfishness which we call by the polite name of "human nature." Jesus said, "Be ye therefore perfect as your Father is perfect." He did not mean perfect in intellectual achievements. He said, "Your Father is utterly impartial; he pours rain on the just and on the unjust. Be perfect like that in impartiality and unselfishness and love."

When one man acts selfishly, those whom he mistreats will feel resentment, and that, too, is a sin. For resentment is hate. It is much easier for us to be unselfish than not to have resentment toward those who are selfish.

So selfishness and resentment are always found together. And in these two sins are found at least half of the blockings that keep God out of life.

We may not rush in and take advantage of somebody else. We may not belong to the "grab-it-first" type. There is a more subtle form of selfishness. This is to avoid discomfort by staying away from calls of need. This is the selfishness of "refined" people. Never in history have people been more fond of comforts than they are now. Luxuries which were not possible for kings and princes of old are now commonplace for us. Our comforts tempt us to refuse to help the neediest people in the world, if it means sacrificing our comforts. Or if we do give up those comforts we pity ourselves.

VI

SAINTS GET BLOCKED, TOO!

MANY PEOPLE TELL US OF SHARP DISAPPOINTMENT SOON after they have had a great spiritual experience. This happens after revival meetings so often that some people are bitterly opposed to all revivals. They say that the reaction is bad.

The trouble is not with the revival, but with something else. I believe it is because our bucket is filled up, and there is no room for more. We begin to coast along on the memory of a wonderful experience, and it turns bad, like manna in the wilderness or like milk left in a pail.

The spirit of God is like gasoline in a tank of an automobile or an airplane. It is of no use unless it is harnessed to accomplish something. If you have had a spiritual experience and it is slipping from your grasp, if you look up toward heaven and heaven seems deaf, then stop looking toward heaven and look toward humanity. You can't have a great spiritual experience again until you have given the one you *do* have to someone else. That may mean sacrifice. It may mean moving out of your comfortable home. It may mean going where there is great need. Many a man who had been going dry spiritually has gone down to the slums and found Christ waiting for him there, and his soul has soared once more.

In the Roman Catholic Church and in all the literature

71

of mysticism one of the most common phrases we find is "spiritual dryness." Pious people prayed to heaven, and heaven seemed deaf and dumb. The literature of piety is full of explanations of this; it says that even Jesus on the cross cried, "My God, my God, why hast thou forsaken me?" and that God forsakes us as a sort of spiritual discipline.

I think that is not the real reason. I believe it is because people forgot human need and so had stopped the flow downward. I believe it is because buckets cannot contain the Holy Spirit. Only pipe lines open at both ends can hold the Spirit. Any man to whom heaven seems deaf and dumb should not look toward heaven, but toward the bottom of his bucket; then kick the bottom out! The pipe line is not wide open until the opening out toward humanity is as big as the opening up toward God. The pipe line is as large as its smallest diameter.

Heaven is neither deaf nor empty. All the resources of the universe are there, ready to be poured on the world. But we hold the faucet in our hands. God says: "Ho, every one that thirsteth, come . . ." We decide, and yet the law of God's giving is that "you cannot have it unless you give it away." This is the meaning of so many of the sayings of Jesus: "Give, and it shall be given running over. . . ."

The water of life will flow *to* us only if it flows *through* us. You can't keep it unless you give it away. You can't even have it. The greatest thing in the world changes color and taste even while you hold it. Let go of it quickly—pass it on. God is love, and love is what pours through. Love does not mean self-love. The moment a man tries to keep God to himself he ceases to have love; he has only self-love. Love is love only if it passes on. So all any saint who is suffering from spiritual dryness needs is to open a wide outlet of self-giving service.

The Salvation Army lassies never write books about

spiritual dryness, for they reach downward as well as upward. They are radiant as the glory of God passes through them to where it is needed. "He that receives the water that I shall give him will be a well of water. . . . Out of him shall flow rivers of living water."

It is easier to love God than to love people. The God we see in Jesus Christ is the most lovable person in the universe —but *people* are often contemptible. We must school ourselves to love people because they need love and not because they are attractive. As a matter of fact, the people who need us most are those whom others do not love at all. They are likely to be irritating. They are often bad-mannered and bad-tempered. They may be dirty and bad smelling. In my own work among illiterates I have learned that one must forget dirty clothes and bad smells and rough manners and see only the soul, with its pathetic need, behind the repulsive and sometimes bestial human façade.

One of the problems of those who seek the good life is that the closer they draw to God, the more clearly they see the sins and weaknesses of human nature. And the greatest temptation of one who is trying to be a Christian is to be critical of those who do not share his Christian ideals. So it is often said that the hardest man to live with is a saint! The fault of a saint is his unforgiving and critical nature, sometimes his cruel tongue. How to hate wrong, yet feel love and tolerance for one who does wrong is a problem every Christian must face. This problem does not grow less; it grows greater as one's dedication to God increases.

A great many saints are blocked also because they try to hold God to only one channel. For example, the Roman Catholic Church seldom appreciates any saint except one who has been canonized by the Catholic Church.

My Baptist friends have admitted that they appreciate and talk about the achievements of Baptists more than those of other denominations. This goes to a greater or lesser extent for every denomination.

We all tend to shut ourselves out from God's myriad channels because we insist on God flowing down through our particular denominational or social or political channel. The dryness of many a saint has resulted from his closing off every pipe line except one. It is dreadful how sectarianism makes men consider goodness sinful unless if flows down their own ecclesiastical ditch! To be perfectly fair, I suppose I am as prejudiced as others, *unconsciously*. We are all plagued with blind areas. We can see the specks in other eyes but not in our own. We do not see our own sins.

And inability to discriminate between what is good and what is just narrow prejudice is the block of many saints. Jesus said it was a sin to put up barriers of custom and make them more sacred than the laws of God.

> The love of God is broader
> Than the measure of man's mind
> And the heart of the eternal
> Is most wonderfully kind.

The little "I don't like this!" whispered in every direction frustrates God, and He must discover some way— if He can—to get past us to get His will done in spite of our silent rebellion. We start by not liking the weather, and that is the one thing for which God is solely responsible.

Glenn Clark's little pamphlet, *The Divine Plan*, is so good that every saint ought to memorize it. Dr. Clark believes that every instant of the day *every incident that arises* is God's best answer to our need *at that particular moment*. He who is willing to listen to God, no matter from what direction God speaks, will never know spiritual dryness. The greatest and highest lesson to learn is to say yes to the God who is speaking forever and forever in six billion ways!

One reason it is so difficult to say yes is that God's voice upsets our own previous intentions. You and I struggle between two things, both of which are right—the right which we had planned to do and the right which it seems to us God is telling us to do now. We plan a morning in which to do very important work, and a stranger interrupts us. He needs help; *and need is the voice of God*. But you and I are tempted to get rid of him as quickly as possible, so that we can carry out *our* plans.

These are not the sins and trials of bad people. They are the sins and trials of the best people. The more conscientious we are, the more we struggle between the better and the best. The saints are constantly plagued by the question, "How do I know this voice is God's? How do I know that this idea at this present moment is not a device of the devil to block the work that needs to be done?" How do I know that the devil has not blocked this book month after month because he wants it frustrated? What is the answer to that question?

Is this the answer: that God gives us judgment and expects us to use our judgment to decide when the devil tempts us? Are we to use our best judgment and then have faith that that is His Voice? The commonest of all questions that we ask ourselves is, "How can I *know*, so that I will not make a mistake?" I suspect that these questions remain unanswered in order that we may be trained in judgment. For we are being trained to be sons of God, and good sense is a characteristic of the good son of God.

You can't be sure all the time; you have to guess. But in my own life and experience I find that if I guess while praying, my guess is usually right. I believe it is a pretty safe policy to say, "God help me to guess right," and then to go ahead. Men and women who have big responsibilities in this world have to make decisions and stand by them.

There is one thing that we are not free to do. We are not free to decide whether to do God's will or disobey it. After the decision to join the family of God has been made, the only question we have to answer is, "What is God's will?" He doesn't always tell us, at least not at the time we want to be told. He waits while we ponder and weigh, and the very pondering and weighing, if we are praying at the same moment, makes us stronger Christians, just as a hard problem helps a boy in school to become a better mathematician.

There is a deep reason why many of our questions remain unanswered for some time. The greatest and wisest thing any human being ever does is to pray to God. When you are talking to God you are doing the last supreme thing God wants of you. In eternity we shall be talking with God all the time. So God leaves us groping for answers *because God wants us to keep on praying. The prayer is far more important than the answer.*

In a Camp Farthest Out a woman told me that there was just one request she had to make of God, and then she would be satisfied. That was that she might actually see Jesus. I thought this request would have been more beautiful if she had longed for all the world to see Jesus. Wanting more for yourself than you want for others may be "human," but it is not divine. One finds people forever longing for some more wonderful experience for their own satisfaction; they thoughtlessly assume that God will reward them with blessings others cannot have.

From beginning to end, Jesus rejected the temptation to use His gifts for himself. In the wilderness when He was tempted to take things for Himself He said no three times. "Make bread for yourself," was the temptation to seek His own comfort. No! "Jump from the pinnacle of the temple," was the temptation to become prominent. No! "All the nations will be given you if you compromise," was the temptation to use His power. No! There in the wilderness Jesus decided that He did not live to satisfy self. He had one obligation: *endless compassionate service*. He hewed to that line all the rest of His life.

If He turned water into wine, it was to serve. If He calmed the storm, it was to serve. If He made five loaves feed five thousand, it was to serve. If He opened blind eyes or raised the dead, it was always the measureless love of God in service. He never did anything to amaze people nor to frighten them, nor to serve Himself. On the cross His enemies wagged their fingers at Him and said, "He saved others; himself he cannot save." That was one of the truest things ever spoken about Jesus. Those men had seen in Him just what He had wanted them to see. He had revealed that side of God which no one else would ever have thought of revealing. God stays out of sight while He saves others; He hides Himself and gets His joy out of seeing people unfold the best they have in them. God loves to save others; He has no interest in saving Himself.

The saint is not a saint until he ceases to desire comfort or notoriety or power. And one of the blockages of many a person who is saintly in other regards may be his desire to bask in the limelight.

The ultimate test of a saint is his willingness voluntarily to take up a cross and suffer and die, just as Jesus did.

"Why," you ask, "was it necessary for Jesus to endure that agony?" Perhaps it was necessary in order that all of us might be *sure* that Jesus understands how *we* suffer. He was made perfect in understanding of human misery through His own suffering.

1 Peter 3:19 says that right after the crucifixion Jesus "went and preached unto the spirits in prison." Perhaps Jesus

had to go through hell to understand what hell is. Hell is
separation from God. When Jesus cried "My God, My God,
why has thou forsaken me?" He experienced hell. Most of
us in this world are so accustomed to hell that we don't know
we are in hell until heaven pours in and pushes hell out.
Hell and heaven are both inside of us before we are inside of
them. Hell is inside of us when Christ is outside of us.

I met a beautiful, saintly woman who was bedridden.
She was a very rich woman. Her faith in God was serene on
the surface. And yet she had doctors to treat her for a dozen
diseases. I suspected that the best way for her to be cured was
to forget herself and think of other people in need. I talked
to her about the millions who were worse off than she was,
both sick and miserably poor. But she became impatient with
me, and immediately returned to her own troubles. I believe
if that woman had been able to give away her wealth and to
think about other people, she would have been made well.
With all her piety she was selfish; she wanted God to make
her well, while she remained completely indifferent to a
world in agony.

I know another woman with a like saintly face, but she
was different. Her thought and effort are directed toward
helping people in need. She works hard all the time, and
travels everywhere; she uses her talents and her money for
other people, and she is radiantly healthy. The spirit of God
pours in and through and out, unhindered and in perfect
rhythm. It never makes her ill. It makes her gloriously beautiful and well. Many who read this page will guess her name
—Mrs. Harper Sibley.

So here is a law for the saints: *Don't open the gate too
wide toward heaven unless it is opened equally wide toward
the lowliest and the neediest.* Where the spirit of God is
blocked, it becomes spiritual indigestion; it ceases to be real

love and becomes conflict. Never ask God to give you more than you want Him to give to others.

I realize that this is not the writing of our "sweetness and light" school. It sounds more like the ancient prophets. Too many false modern prophets are saying, "God is good to us, no matter what we do with His goodness." But I think we need to go back to the plain realism of the ancient prophets: "It is an awful thing to fall into the hands of the Living God," as you do when you try to keep Him for yourself. God cannot stomach luxurious religiosity. If you really want to find God give everything away, and give yourself away. That is *exactly* what Jesus said.

Success is dangerous for saints, because success always tempts them to self-esteem, which leads to hypocrisy. Many a man, in what he supposes to be a higher office, softens his message. He finds reasons for living in luxury; he becomes an unconscious *sincere* hypocrite. Few are the preachers in the United States who do not have to fight that battle. More money, more popularity, more success—these are the rewards they get for toning down and sweetening the Gospel. I think the hardest thing in the world is to keep utterly free from unconscious hypocrisy.

One last blockage of the saint is that often he doesn't feel in the *mood* to seek God. He would prefer for a time not to be bothered with religion. All of us are swept back and forth by our moods. We feel like reading something serious at times; at other times we may crave a mystery story. Sometimes it isn't quite that simple. We may claim that it is just a desire for variety when it is actually yielding to an impulse in our lives that we know He would condemn, if we were to ask Him. If we turn to Him and place the thought honestly before Him, He might require something less congenial of us, and so we do not raise the question we conveniently forget! We agree that Jesus listened to God all the time, but we just don't want to be quite *that* perfect.

What are we to do with these "out-of-the-mood" periods? Can't we let up just once in a while? To put it sharply, should we pray when we don't feel like it?

Of course, if we ask God that question, He will answer us quickly. We need prayer *most* when we feel the least like it. Feeling that we are not "in the mood" is not an excuse.

All of us know that when we start a new habit we don't like it at first. But if we persevere, we will at last enjoy what at first we disliked. The lack of an inclination toward God is not a misfortune to which we must surrender; it is a misfortune which we must remedy. It is like a lesson in school. Rather, it *is* a lesson in school, preparing us for membership in the Divine family.

One of the lessons that we all have to learn is to do the thing that at times we don't like to do, and to reject the thing we want to do. Paul put it this way: "Evil is close at hand. I do what I do not want. I do the very thing I hate."

And all of us in our secret hearts know that no matter how we have disciplined ourselves, we must admit that "evil is close at hand." Paul cried, "Wretched man that I am, who will deliver me?" And there came the only answer there is: "Thanks be to God through Jesus Christ our Lord!" —He forgives and He delivers.

So we all need to pray: "Lord, I depend entirely on Thy saving grace to forgive me. I have found out that I cannot do right without Thy help."

> "Just as I am without one plea,
> But that Thy blood was shed for me,
> And that Thou bid'st me come to Thee
> O Lamb of God, I come."

The purpose of this chapter was to discuss the blockages of saints, but at the end of it we find that *there are no saints*. All of us alike are sinners. As Reinhold Neibuhr said, "Nobody but sinners can get into the Kingdom of heaven. The 'righteous' cannot get in."

VII

BREAKING THE LOG JAM

MODERN MEDICINE SAYS THAT SUSCEPTIBILITY TO DISEASE results from an imbalance of hormones. We all know this is true of diabetes, but the doctors say it is also probably true of all other noncontagious diseases. Our new knowledge also tells us that hormones are stimulated or repressed by our thoughts. Therefore, the disease behind the disease may be an unbalanced thought life.

When we think of the various blockages we have just studied, we will see that some people have too many hormones overworked by self-assertion. Some people have the exact opposite—too great a sense of inferiority and defeatism is *repressing* their hormones. Nine-tenths of the blockages we studied in Chapter V were due to one of those two things, and they were about equally divided. One group was anxious to *rule,* and so they resisted both their God and other people. The other group was afraid they would be *hurt* by other people or by God. Both of these extremes were possessed by a nervous anxiety about themselves because they had no faith in God.

Jesus' command, "Do not be anxious about anything," can be fulfilled only if we are *sure* of God. So we see where the release must come. Something must happen to strengthen our faith in God. That something happens through Jesus Christ, and I want to make very clear exactly why.

In most religions and in many sects of Christianity people are frightened at the thought of the power and majesty and goodness and righteousness of God. People may pray to God, but still be afraid of Him, because they misunderstand Him. They think He is watching to catch them and punish them; they think of Him as the Supreme Judge of the universe, in fact, as both Judge and Policeman. All over the world there are people who have been so nervously frightened at the judgment of God that religion has not cured them of their blockages, but only blocked them further. St. Paul said that that was what the Jewish Law was for; he said it was to pile up sins so high that we became hopeless. And then, said Paul, "Jesus Christ came, and through him the glorious assurance that God forgives and forgets everything in our past; forgives it, forgets it, and cures it." Through Jesus Christ, and through Him only, do I find that the world dares to approach God without fear.

Jesus said, "Stop being frightened. God knows you are bad. He knows it is because you are weak that you fall so often. He forgives you. He wants you to start over." The greatest thing ever said about God is that He has as much love as Jesus Christ. Christ has raised our opinion of God. God is a better God than we thought He could be. We, of course, never would have dared to breathe our low opinion of God. We were too much frightened that He would strike us dead for blasphemy. Now that we know Jesus, we dare even say that we had not realized God could be so good.

At the Camp Farthest Out at Winnipesaukee 699 people reported releases from their blockages.

178 releases were centered in Jesus Christ.

160 said that by an effort of will they turned from sin.

158 said that they got a new love for humanity.

99 said they were released by the help of other people.

94 said it was a glorious emotional experience.

More interesting than these statistics are the radiant testimonials that these released people gave:

I suffered from two diseases, one spiritual, the other physical: extreme self-itis and arthritis. I felt jealousy, possessiveness and resentment that others shared the friendship of my friend. I pitied myself. I could not walk for pain.

At the camp I told my friend my story. We prayed together. I became so full of the Holy Spirit that I got up and walked. The pain had entirely gone. My friend and I went to the prayer-room; there we rededicated ourselves and left the problem with God. Now I have joy, love, peace.

Another was "tied up by hate":

I was resentful of little slights and full of hate, caught in bitterness. A woman who had been tied up by hate told me how she prayed and heard the answer: "Give it all to Him."

That rang the bell with me. So when I began to hate again, I stopped and said, "God, take this *away*," and He took it! Now, every day, when hate begins to return, I say, "God, take it away," and it goes instantly. I never imagined this was possible. It is truly amazing.

To me the most heart-warming, touching releases of all were those of a group of 178 people who surrendered to Jesus Christ. I am putting them together in one group because I realize that it is almost too sweet, almost too wonderful, to believe. And yet I suppose that if God gave us the power to look into all the hearts of His loving children at one time we would get the same impression that you would get from these people: "too good to be true, almost too sweet to be endured."

I believe that somewhere on this page any reader who has been in quest of God will find a note that will start his own soul singing.

Here is a heart-wringing testimony:

I hated my husband for his infidelity. I hated the children he had by another woman. I hated all men. I wanted to die.

I came to the CFO, and there I saw Glenn Harding's face. I saw every face radiating kindness. I went to the prayer-room every day. I could not pray for myself, so I prayed for others. While the tears rolled down my cheeks, I surrendered. I tried to forgive, tried hard. And then came release. I felt twenty pounds lighter. My cold disappeared at once. The tension left my body. I fell asleep. I wanted to go back to my husband and babies. No words can describe the relief. I had given God the burden. Now I can smile at people and love them and trust men again. I can talk and pray aloud. All this the camp did for me.

Here is another:

I was full of pride and vanity, close to a nervous breakdown. I was afraid of every sound and of every person. This fear was hell on earth. Irritations and resentments and annoyances came all day to torment me.

Then I read *Health Through Prayer* and *You Are My Friends*. I was reborn. Last evening I lost all my fear and pride and resentments. I was washed in the love which floods the camp. Christ's spirit is hovering like a dove over me. Each day I see my channels clearing. . . . Now I face the world afraid of nothing. I am ready for a Pentecost. Now I know that God is always doing His best.

And from another:

I was blocked because I could not believe that Jesus was the Son of God. At the CFO I had a glorious vision of Christ in the skies, twice. Now I know. He lives for me, He is real. He is Jesus Christ, the Son of God. I am born again to the dear Jesus. His love and joy are passing through to bless others. He tells me what to read in the Bible. He opens my ears to listen to the radio; He talks to me through my friends. He goes with me on shopping tours; He stretches my pennies in an amazing way. He lets me meet wonderful friends; nothing is too trivial for Him to share. He gives me an inner peace, a creative silence. He has brought me life.

And still another:

My mind was closed to the Bible. The church did me no good. My heart was full of scorn. Then my only brother went to the war. I had to pray then: "God, if there be a God, teach me to believe that you will care for my brother."

I wrote a long letter to my brother at the front. Then I held it up and asked God to help my brother get that letter. Then I fell back weeping; I did not know why. Three months later I learned why I had wept. My brother was killed that day. That is how God took care of him. God is taking sweet care of my brother ever since—and of me.

Here is another confession which says what many would like to say:

I built my own blockades of impatience, intolerance, criticism, sarcasm, bitter, stinging tongue, and this was followed by physical and mental illness. The blocks were tremendous and seemed immovable.

In my dark hour I reached out my hand saying: "Do you love Jesus?" And I answered myself, "Yes, I do."

"Do you love Him enough for any sacrifice; can you give up all, even self, for Him?"

As I asked it, I felt a love around me; and I wanted to hug the world. I said, "Lord Jesus, I give you myself completely, and I beg you never to leave me." A light shone brilliantly around me, and His love washed my blocks away.

And here from fifty people are some of the sweetest stories ever told:

I turned in surrender to God and rose above human fear.

In a vision at CFO Christ said, "Follow me," and in great tenderness He took my hand.

I just felt the block melt!

Christ came between me and the storm, and I felt a great calm.

I had been afraid of every sound, of every person, but last night in bed I felt His spirit come in. Tears of joyous thanksgiving flowed, and now I am afraid of nothing.

I was with people full of the love of God until I caught their radiance, joy, faith.

Overwhelming joy of awareness.

God waited, and when I at last invited, He poured through and worked His miracle.

I clasped my Bible to my breast like a breastplate. I held it up and asked God to help me. Then I fell backwards and wept. God had answered.

I just decided to trust Him and stop trying to conquer alone. My weakness yielded to His ability.

I ventured to pray for the throat condition of another, and he was healed. Now I know!

I have begun to have secret trysts with Christ.

I hated myself, and I asked Him to make me all over into a new person.

My fear of people and of failure was drowned in an ocean of love.

I loved everybody and feared nobody.

I have heard His voice and felt His touch, and I had a strong desire to be His instrument.

My loved one was dead, and through my anguish I looked to God. There came a holy, peaceful joy, and earth's cares dropped off. I shall never be alone again. My loved one is with Christ.

I started praying for father, mother, stepmother, sisters, sisters-in-law, neighbors, each by name, and when I prayed, I loved. I was sure He answered my prayer.

He erased me.

Now I feel Christ's love and with it exquisite joy and release and peace.

Christ spoke to me today, and He was wonderful.

My channel broke open and Christ came in.

His love is flowing constantly. This kind of joy is new.

A new life is starting in me like a newly conceived child.

A friend with a lovely voice stepped right inside my heart with Christ.

I found that though I can't, *He can!*

I saw that nothing on earth can really hurt me if I have Christ.

Christ called me to dare to go all the way with Him and to take not one step without Him.

I overcame during the All Night of Prayer.

I laid my defeated self on the offering plate during the church service, and He smiled at me.

I feel as though my whole inner self had been wind-swept, Father, by your Holy Spirit: a lightness within, a quiet trust. Thank God, I am born again.

Here is a testimony so touching that it must be told in full:

Blind at fifty, blind since birth. In utter, impenetrable darkness. Not even the tiniest sliver of light could pass through the massive stone wall which sealed in the oppressive pall. The wall reached beyond the sky and surrounded me completely. And the tragedy of it all was my inability to realize that there was any obstruction. To my mind I could see perfectly and was entirely oblivious of any barrier. I had no needs; there was no want that could not be satisfied. Of wordly goods I had an ample supply. I was entirely self-satisfied. Not a bad situation to find oneself in at the age of fifty—I was secure.

How blind I was! What a fool to think that material security was sufficient! But the Lord does not neglect even the blind. One of His witnesses managed somehow to work a tiny opening through the great wall and the needle-like ray, small though it was, reduced the darkness to such a degree as to cause a blinking and a realization that here was a potent power that my life had never known before. How wonderful it was! How different everything appeared! How it filled me and disclosed new vistas! What a glow came over me! Could it be that my fifty years had been spent in a fool's paradise? I must learn more. I worked at the tiny opening until it admitted more light. It required a little effort, but the results were electrifying. I was bathed in a radiant light. My mind, my body, and my spirit were a tingle. I was walking on air. Sensations I had never realized existed became manifest.

I had entered His Kingdom. For fifty years my channels had been collecting debris. The saturation point had been reached. There was no penetration. But a miracle made an opening, and He entered as through the small end of a funnel, increasing and expanding until I was entirely submerged in His glorious, cleansing light. The clogged channel had been cleared.

Now, at fifty-three, I have been transformed. I am in Him

and He in me. My security is in Him. Material things have come and gone, but that does not disturb me, for I am secure in His love! He is my shepherd, and I shall not want.

Blind at fifty but all-seeing at fifty-three! Dead at fifty but reborn again!

As we read these vivid, intimate stories of blockages and release, they sound like water piling up behind a dam, higher and higher, until the dam breaks. And what is piling up behind us is trouble, suffering, disappointment and failure.

God puzzles us when He allows these things. We are lazy toward Him as well as toward the world. Our obsession in this civilized age of gadgets is to get more and more conveniences and comforts. Men invent conveniences of every sort and sell them to us without much trouble, because they save us from moving. We are trying to find a way to be comfortable and to take it easy; that is the motive behind most people's quest for money. They work hard now so that they can retire later.

But God has no such plan for us. I may be wrong, but I believe we will never retire in heaven on a pension. So far as we can see, God has been wooing the microbe and the worm and the reptile and the mammal and mankind upward. And so, in spite of our refrigerators and sleep-inducing mattresses, God will find a way to make us rise to a new level.

In his book, *The Meaning of History*, Arnold Toynbee is talking for God when he says, "The law of the universe is: Rise to a new level or perish." But God does not let us perish; He just lets us suffer. Until we long for something better than we have or are, God can do nothing. And the moment we hunger or thirst, God can fill us. Desire throws open the door of the soul, and then we feel the Divine invasion. Then comes an elation like that we feel when we have been off on a long journey and get back home with those we love, or like the elation of a young man who feels that at last he has found the woman for whom he has always been looking. It is falling in love—in love with God, in love with Christ.

One woman at a Camp Farthest Out wrote this letter to God:

> CFO Camp Warren
> Benton Harbor, Michigan
> September 17, 1948

Dear God:

I am your open channel to work through. From this time forth you are my one and only contact. I look to you for all guidance. I surrender my life to you. Tell me what you want me to do next. Work through me as you worked through Jesus your Son.

Help me to erase self and become selfless. Dear God, give me the power to heal Thy children. Make me more like Thy son Jesus, day by day. Fill me with Thy Divine Love.

Ever listening for your command.

> Your patient child,
> Vera

It is a love different from any love we ever had before. It shouldn't be called by the same name. Human love is the love of people because they are lovable, because they are attractive. But divine love is the love of people for their own sakes. It doesn't look at people first and love them afterwards. It doesn't ask what satisfaction or comforts those other persons can give. It loves people, not because they are attractive, but because they are in need, not because they are lovable, but because they need loving; not because it wants anything from them but because it wants to give everything to them. It isn't love in the ordinary sense of the word.

There are no words to express it except "the love of Christ."

The soul that is transformed by this love is aware not only of a heaven but also of a hell that must be made heaven.

Somewhere in this world, every second of every day, this miracle of a changed life by the invasion of God is happening. That alone is the hope of the world, as it is the hope of every soul. We are witnessing now the chain reaction of the love of Christ, which is doing the same thing to the human race that the atoms do to one another in an atom bomb. And it will continue until this hell which we call earth is changed into heaven, and His Kingdom has come.

VIII

LEARNING TO WALK WITH GOD

We are trying an experiment: we are in this book, calling on God and listening for an answer and letting experience tell us whether it works. It is as justifiable an experiment as any experiment in science. And it is like all psychological experiments; it must be worked out in the laboratory of our own minds and souls.

Nearly everything in the Christian religion is experimental. We rightly call it an "experimental religion." It starts with authorities whose wonderful lives and deep integrity makes us admire and trust them; we see in them more radiant and wonderful lives than other people have, and we want to be like them. We ask them why they are this way, and they tell us they got it from Jesus Christ and the Father. We want to live that way, so we try getting in touch with God to see whether it works with us.

Before a scientist tries an experiment, he must have faith in the work of those who already have reported success.

That is all the faith we need in order to begin our experiment with "divine imagination." We know that imagination precedes everything that any man ever creates. As Plato told us a long time ago, "Ideas are architectonic"; they are pregnant and they begin to become reality. So, for a better world, we need more people holding better thoughts.

Again, we know that when we listen, our highest imagination seems to be something better than we are. It seems like something from God. You do not know this when you begin, but you come to understand it as your experiment progresses. I did; I know you will. A greater number of people every day are finding that this kind of experimental religion takes them far beyond where scientists who are out of contact with God have ever gone.

He who pursues this experiment with the spirit finds that his years are like an ever-enlarging funnel. This is the testimony of the saints who have gone before us. If you have done any experimenting with God, I think you have found as I did, that *so far as you have gone,* the saints have told the truth. And no matter how far you go, you will still find that it is better all the way along. This is why the faces of some dear old saints fairly shine with glory.

The hymn "Take Time to Be Holy," expresses the hardest thing we have to do in the dedicated life. We must take time from the crowding voices and interests of life. We shall not "find" time; we shall have to "take" it! We shall have to take it away from other demands which crowd and press on us. Many of us have to take it off our sleeping time. If we do, I think we need not feel too much worry about lost sleep. Those who take time from their sleep to pray say that they get as much refreshment from their fellowship with God as though they were asleep. Business men may find it necessary to take from three o'clock to five o'clock in the morning, or from four o'clock to six o'clock in the morning, before other people are up and around. A housewife may find it necessary to take the time after her husband has gone to work and the children have gone to school. Or it may be necessary to take time from your leisure.

This devotional hour is beset by temptations. The devil tries to ruin it. We have to take time by violence. Jesus said:

"The kingdom of heaven cometh by violence, and men take it violently." Whatever that means, it applies to our devotions. We have to know that our walk with God is *priority Number One*. Feeding on God is as necessary for the spiritual life as eating our meals is for our physical life. Bible study and prayer are the bread and meat of the spirit life. Many of us find that we have to *fight for our lives* if we want to keep alive spiritually.

Even the good things that call for your time are bad if they crowd out this sacred time with Christ. The good is often the enemy of the best. Even when we try to do good we shall not do it unless we are full of His Spirit. We rob the effectiveness of our work and we rob the joy of our life if we rob ourselves of that time to look undisturbed into the face of God.

You should keep on trying various ways of spending that hour until you find the way that best meets your particular need. It seems that there are almost as many ways as there are people.

Some people use that hour best when they are praying with others.

Some sit with a pencil and paper and write out what God seems to give them.

Some try to make their minds a total blank and commune in silence, like the Quakers, for an hour.

Some like to get off alone and talk *aloud* to God about their problems, and about how they love Him and about everything else.

Some allow their tongues to talk back to them, saying what their imagination tells them God would say.

Some keep a prayer list.

Some discipline themselves to write an ever-longer list of names of persons for whom they are lifting up intercessory prayer.

Some pray and then write letters to people as they feel led of God to write them.

Some read devotional books like *The Upper Room,* or any of the hundreds of others. Some read books about the life of Jesus, such as *The Greatest Story Ever Told.*

Some people find the best devotion in playing a piano, or singing prayer hymns.

Some wait, perhaps, with pen in hand for God to tell them what to do next. The Moslems pray with their faces to the floor. Many Christians pray on their knees. Many pray before pictures of Jesus, many before a cross.

Any method, absolutely any method is *your* method if you find it opens the doors toward heaven and helps you gain close contact with God. And it is not *your* method, no matter who does it, if it does not succeed in doing that.

A devotional hour is no substitute for "constantly abiding," but it is an indispensible help; it starts the day right.

But the day must be kept right. We should cultivate the habit of turning to God whenever we stop any piece of work and look around to ask what to do next. Those little interim moments are priceless.

It is not necessary to pray long prayers; a fraction of a second is enough. It is a wonderful thing to shoot silent flash prayers at people whom we meet. If we are sitting in a church or a railroad train, it is good to pray for the people who are around us. It is good to cultivate the habit of taking walks with God. It is good to talk to Him when dressing, when in the bathroom. We can be whispering to our Father as we fall asleep in bed. When we awaken in the morning or lean back to rest on our chair for a moment we can talk with Him. Everyone of these moments can be a time for recharging our spiritual batteries.

The great prayer masters devoted all, or nearly all, of their waking hours to prayer. That does not mean that they

did nothing else; it means that they prayed and worked si-
multaneously. They prayed while they read, while they
walked, while they listened to music, while they were writing, while they were working with their hands. They shared
all they did and all they thought and all they said with God,
and thus they could engage in a busy life and yet "pray without ceasing."

One person protested to me that this discipline of
prayer seems not to be natural. Of course, it is not natural.
But that is nothing against it. Cooking is not natural. Our
remote ancestors ate raw meat and cooked nothing. Neither
are clothes natural, nor knives, nor forks. Natural people go
unclothed and eat with their hands. It is not natural to become like Jesus Christ. It is more than natural. It may be
called supernatural. But that is no argument at all against it.
You may argue that a thing is unhealthful or unwhole-
some, but to argue that it is against nature is not to argue
against it but to argue in its favor. We all want to rise above
the nature of our ancestors and the nature of the beast. We
must rise, if we are to become full-grown sons of God, and
there is no way to rise higher than we were without struggle.

When one first tries to form this new habit, his mind
resists and runs off on a tangent. This stage of mind wan-
dering must be endured by all who would learn this discipline. It is true of every new good habit that one seeks to
form. We must pass through a period of failure. But we need
not feel discouraged when we fail, for if we persevere we
shall at last see growth. This learning to live with God is the
highest of all habits. It is the greatest advancement that the
human animal has made. It may take longer to form than
any other habit, but after a while experience will show that
it grows easier. After months and years of practicing the
presence of God, one feels that God is closer; His push from

behind seems to be stronger and steadier, and the pull from in front seems to grow stronger, and the goal does not seem quite so far away.

At last, God gets so close that one stops thinking of God as outside himself, and begins to think of Christ inside in one's own thought and breast. He sees God's thoughts flow into his mind. Sometimes one feels that they are coming in from above but more often one feels that these thoughts are welling up from the unconscious, as from a hidden fountain. God is so close then that He not only lives all around us, but all *through* us. And this is exactly the way God wants it to be.

As one continues to practice this presence of God, his thoughts seem to grow progressively better, more fruitful than they were when he began. Some people give it up because at first it produces only a few scattered thoughts, and they seem not to be very valuable. It is like changing over on the typewriter from the one finger "hunt-and-peck method" to the touch system; anyone who has tried that knows that it is not easy. The old way keeps breaking in on the new. So it is with stopping this desultory, foggy, contact with God which we have been practicing, as we strive for a "constant abiding."

The rewards are beyond description. In the first place, perpetual prayer produces an immense change in the way we think. We learn to ask God to think His thoughts in us. This attempt to share His thoughts will mean that we will also share His work. Instead of telling God what we want from Him, we ask Him what He wants *us* to do.

It also transforms the way we look at people. Until He takes over we look at them to decide whether we like or dislike them, whether they attract us or leave us cold. But when God thinks in us, the thoughts we think about other people are not determined by whether they are attractive but by how much they need. Our first question is whether we can do anything for them.

When we pray for other people, sharing God's thought means we surrender those people to the will of God. We do not ask Him to heal them or to improve them but to get His will done in them.

This kind of communion can go on aloud, if there is no one near us who will be disturbed. Or it can go on in the deep silence of our souls. After a while, we can learn to commune with our Lord silently no matter how large the crowd around us.

God tells us what to pray for when we are thus open to Him. St. Paul saw this when he said, "We do not know how to pray as we ought, but the Spirit himself intercedes for us." Julian of Norwich said this same thing in his poem in which he imagines God speaking. God says:

> "First, it is my will that you have it,
> Then I make thee to will it,
> I make thee to beseech it
> And thou beseechest it."

When we are open enough, we ask what God first suggests to us, and then, when we hear His suggestion, that is what we ask. God never denies any request if we have first asked Him what His request is, for then we have not changed His will, but *He has changed ours*. Letting God tell us what we shall think and ask makes a great deal of difference. For example let us examine this prayer. Is it listening only to God?

"God, I am confronted with the necessity of preparing a sermon for tomorrow. Guide my thinking so that it will be good for the people to hear."

Is that praiseworthy? No. It's better than nothing, but

it isn't the finest prayer. For I told God what I wanted Him to do for me this next hour. A perfect surrender would have begun this way:

"Lord, what do you want me to share with you now? What shall we think or do together?" It is the difference between asking God to help us and asking God how we can help Him.

You might reply that God might tell us not to prepare our sermon at all. Well, if God does not agree with us that the sermon needs to be prepared, He is all-wise, is He not? We would have to trust Him, in that case. And when we do trust Him, so far as my experience is concerned, He never lets us down. That, however, is something which other people must test for themselves. Then they must testify after they have tested it. If God is like Christ and if that sermon needs to be written, He will tell us about the sermon. But meanwhile we gave God an opportunity to decide *whether* it is to be a sermon or not. I hope this shows clearly the dividing line between *half-yielding* to God and *completely* yielding.

Instead of trying to do all his hard *thinking* alone, one should do some hard *listening*. There is a profound difference. If one hands over a difficult problem to God and says, "God, what *is* the answer? I will wait until I hear from you," processes deep down in our unconscious mind begin to operate and God in his own way gives us the answer. No amount of straining or worrying would have given it to us.

What shall we do if we are overcome by sleep when we are praying? There is no reason to struggle against it. Go to sleep. God sends sleep. We will not resist anything that He gives us, from within or from without, not even sleep!

However, if an evil thought comes, we know that God did not send that. That is the devil trying to drown out God's voice. Usually, probably always, we can tell where a thought comes from by *its spiritual quality*. When the thought is evil, we push a little harder to the heart of God, and the evil thought goes.

In this search for God's constant guidance we must be sure we are not pretending, either to God or to ourselves or to others. The higher we reach, the easier it is to become sincere hypocrites! We fool ourselves but not others. People penetrate the least fraud. As for God, He sees the fraud long before we do. Our life must be real, and with a single eye:

"One burning passion, filling all my frame."

It is uncanny the way the subconscious in other people detects any insincerity. I detect it in others. They detect in me any double purpose, any ulterior motive. Nobody really ever fools anybody else for long. Lovely words and even lovely deeds cannot save the man from being detected if his motives are low.

Some of you who read this book may be Christian workers seeking financial aid; you had better remember that the people who have the money know whether you are interested in their purses or in them. You cannot hide your real purpose. I do not think we shall ever need to worry about money if we keep it clear that people *count*. If we are troubled about not having enough money, perhaps God doesn't want us to have it. Our high goal is to be like Christ. That is not something that money can buy. I did not say our highest goal is to be a Christian, if "Christian" means the *average* Christian. That is not half high enough—not one-tenth high enough.

But if we make our aim so high, do we not invite certain failure before we begin? We cannot be like Christ, can we? The answer is, "No, not perfectly." But, we can grow imperfectly, but progressively, toward the fullness of the stature of Christ. Indeed, we are sure to grow if we expose ourselves to Him daily—all day, beginning early in the morning.

But when we try to keep the windows open toward God, we find that with our own strength, as a matter of plain honesty, we cannot do it. Every saint who really tried that has found that he could not do it alone. He needs, and all of us need, Christ inside to keep that window open toward the Father and toward humanity. Unless Christ is within we cannot succeed. We must first invite Him inside, then when He is within, directing our thinking, He keeps the window open upward to God and outward to men. What was once an impossible struggle for us becomes easier than easy. We have no trouble at all; that is, we have no trouble while He is strengthening us.

But we cannot take vacations from God. That is another way of saying that we cannot pull the branch out of the vine and stay away from Him for a while. We can only take vacations *with* God.

Some ministers live on one level during the week and try to work themselves up to another on Saturday or Sunday morning. They live a secular life six days and a sacred life one day. It is a futile effort. Everybody knows that such a minister is a "jobber," lifting his ideas out of other people's books. "Out of the fullness of the heart the mouth speaks," and the price of having that fullness is walking with God when there is nobody to see or to care. The secret of power is not to work oneself up into a tense fervor on Saturday night or Sunday morning, but to speak with composure, with enormous reserves, and with perfect control.

If we can accomplish "constant abiding," there will come times of marvelous mystical experience. One man wrote to me, "I had a wonderful experience while I was writing my life's decision. I looked up and asked:

"Jesus and Father, have these pages pleased you?

"The answer was like a clear voice in my soul:

" 'Yes child, I am thrilled at the resolve you have made. It was for this kind of communion with us that you were created, that all men were created, that the world itself was created. We love you, too, for trying to enlist others in this high resolve.' "

My friend said his soul tingled with ecstasy.

Such an experience has come to all of us when our surrender is sincere, and when we are trying to help other people. But it will not come to us if we try to let it end in ourselves. The tingling joy of the Holy Spirit comes into us only when it flows *through* us to bless others. The minister gets his blessing when he is blessing others. It flows through him to them. Norman Vincent Peale says he preaches to others the sermon he needs himself, and that as he gives it away he gets more out of it than anybody else. This is equally true of a Salvation Army lassie, or of a nurse in a hospital. It is the secret of the spirit life. We get by giving. We lose as soon as we stop giving.

We may be grateful when we get these enormously joyous experiences; grateful too that when we pray, we improve our health. But we must not pray for delightfully mystical sensations, nor in order to keep ourselves physically well. That is not the prayer that God loves. Prayer for others should not be tinged with selfish motives. I doubt that prayer will work if you pray only for yourself. It sounds too much like sanctified selfishness. That kind of prayer can be just as contemptible in God's sight as any other form of self-centeredness. God searches the deep purposes of the heart, and He will be able to make use of our prayer only if it is utterly sincere and utterly free from small motives of any kind. Our purpose must be as pure and selfless as the purpose of Jesus when He said, "For their sakes I sanctify myself, that they also may be sanctified in the truth." When our motive goes far beyond pleasure or health or advantage for self, when it reaches with arms ten thousand miles long to bring the world to Christ, then power flows through and in and out like rivers of living water.

This is the verdict of the saints down through the centuries. We who have gone only a little way know that it is true. And we testify that the other directions we have tried promised us much, but gave us nothing. He only has given us more and more and more than He ever promised.

All the saints in heaven will say, "Amen" to that testimony. For God not only gives more than He promises here, but throughout all the ages to come He will continue to give more than eye has seen or ear has heard or than it has entered into the mind of man to imagine.

IX

HOW TO PRAY FOR OTHERS

PRAYER FOR OTHERS IS THE FIRST, SIMPLEST, MIGHTIEST channel in the world. It is the most unused power on earth today. That we fail to pray enough for others I admit, and I have no doubt you will admit it too.

Why do we neglect it as we do? It is because we place an exaggerated emphasis on ourselves. That is the disease of our age. It is more a disease of our age than it was in any previous age of world history. The ideal of liberty has become confused with self-interest. This tendency carries over into our religion. It reveals itself in our praying as well as in our daily life and in our thinking and our actions.

Listen to any impromptu pulpit prayer in church and ask yourself how much of that prayer is for the people inside your church, and how much of it is for others. You will discover that nine-tenths, or perhaps ten-tenths of the prayer you hear is for "us in this church." The minister will defend himself by saying that he is voicing the heart's desires of the people before him in the pews, that he is ministering to their need.

But, I ask, is that all his people *ought* to desire? Don't they need to pray for others? They are supposed to be grown Christians. They are supposed to be helping God save the world. This prayer that ends in self reveals something that

104

must pain God: it reveals that the people's major obsession is *not to save the world but to save themselves* from their own troubles.

If this is the most altruistic thought they can find even in church, what must our average thinking be? Prayer is not lower than common thought; it represents what we consider to be the noblest thought. In prayer we try to measure up to God's expectations. These church prayers fall far below the selfless grandeur of Christ. They do not as a rule rise above "enlightened self-interest."

Or listen to the preaching year in and year out of many preachers who draw large crowds. These sermons appeal predominantly to the self-interests of the people who come to listen to them. Such preaching, truth be told, is needed badly. The first thing a preacher must do for his people is to help them settle the question that stands between themselves and God.

But doesn't this question between ourselves and God *ever* get settled? Must it be the *last* thing as well as the first thing which obsesses our thoughts? This matter of our own sins in relation to God ought not to engross all of our time or all of our prayer; it ought to be settled so that we can go on to becoming sons and coworkers with God, in prayer as well as in action.

If you feel like throwing this book down and being angry about it, perhaps it is because it touches the one sin all of us try hardest to hide. We find it easy to hide this sin, because we are all caught in it. It is the sin of too much thought about self—the sin of leaving others out or at least leaving out those whom we do not intimately know. We would be still more angry if someone called it "pious selfishness." I think one reason so many people do not pray at all is because they have a guilty feeling that God likes to hear them pray about the things that interest Him most. They, on the other hand, are bored when they pray for others. So they do not pray at all.

Many people suspect religious piety today because it may be a camouflage for selfishness. It is not worse than the situation in the business world, but then the business world does not pretend to be pious or unselfish. Business, at least, is honest about that. Too much of Christianity professes to believe in being unselfish when it is in reality selfish; any ordinary person sees through its shallow hypocrisy. That we are rich and "respectable" blinds us to the fact that in the eyes of heaven we are rather contemptible.

We all tend to become like the Pharisee in the temple who spent his prayer hour thanking God that he was not like other people and spent none of that hour praying for other people. Others could go to hell, so far as he cared. Indeed, it gave him an ugly sense of superiority to think that he was going where they could not go. We loathe his kind. Those sects in the Christian Church and those people in the Christian Church who think that they only will be saved for their orthodoxy, while the rest of us go to hell, do not know they are carrying into their religion the Pharisee's selfish desire to triumph over others. It is all the more loathesome because they are so unctuous about it.

So we are caught between two kinds of self-centeredness —the one secular, the other religious. Our religion is little because we are little. A Moslem leader declared that "sanctified selfishness" was the greatest traitor to Christ still in the Christian Church. But this is changing. The desperateness of our world peril today is giving us a larger concern. We see that we must do something to help our world in order to help ourselves. We see that we cannot survive if our world perishes. So we are beginning to pray for those who can save or ruin the world. I think it is one way in which God is compelling us to get away from our absorption in self and success. It was always true that we could not get into the kingdom of heaven unless we took everybody we could with us. But that truth is hard for people to realize. Today it is easier for people to realize that our world threatens to come crashing around our heads unless we work and pray for other people.

We used to rationalize our selfish prayers by saying that it was useless to pray for other people outside of the Church. This was the common reply when people were asked to pray for political leaders. But today those political leaders are asking the Church by the thousands to pray for them. President Eisenhower is doing that. Every member of Congress wants the prayers of people. So do all the members of our Cabinet, and so do all the leaders of the so-called Christian nations—all of those who belong to a church, and most of those who belong to no church. They want and desperately need devout people to pray for them.

I believe that prayer focused on our world leaders is the most desperately needed thing in the world today. On these leaders rests peace or disaster for the human race. Peace has often depended in the past, and will often depend in the future, on the feelings of anger or fear, on the faith these leaders have. Emotions which the leaders themselves do not understand dominate their action just as much as our emotions dominate *our* actions. The fate of the world might well hinge on our prayers and on our letters conditioning these men to an attitude in which they would seek God's will, and thus get peace and save the world.

In a democracy, the political leaders listen for the voice of the people. Most of the countries in the United Nations call themselves democracies, which means that they have elections, and try to win votes by making friends. Certainly in our own country every Congressman, as well as the President, is trying hard to find out what the will of the people is, and to do it. If they do not find the people's will, it is because the people are silent.

The lobbyists have had such a wonderful opportunity in our government because they are vocal and know how to speak for their clients. There is one way in which every Christian today can be his own lobbyist; this is to pray individually for our leaders and write to them and say that he is praying for them. The Laymen's Movement for a Christian World believed that enough prayer would change our own country's history and perhaps the history of the whole world. So two laymen volunteered to go each day to pray silently during sessions of the United Nations and to talk to the delegates at recess periods, as opportunity afforded. They persuaded the United Nations to open and close with prayer. They succeeded in having a chapel built into the new United Nations Building in New York City. During the sessions of the Assembly in November, 1949, Warren Austin, former United States representative in the United Nations, said that he depended every day on the prayers of these laymen. He sent telephone messages for more and more men to come and pray.

I think the greatest achievement of the United Nations will turn out to be the agreement to help all the backward, hungry people of the world out of their hunger and misery and disease to a decent level of living. That was done during that session when Warren Austin was sending his messages to the Laymen's Movement. By unanimous vote those nations agreed, to the amazement of everybody, that they would co-operate in this new effort to help mankind. The Laymen's Movement, and Warren Austin, believe that this instance of miraculous unanimity in the United Nations, which is seldom unanimous, became possible because the prayers of a very large number of people had prepared the spiritual climate in which the miracle could take place.

The Laymen's Movement publishes the names of all the delegates on a prayer card which is called "Standing in the Need of Prayer." They have had requests for more than one million of these prayer cards. More than 50,000 people have written back to the Laymen's Movement saying they are praying every day for these delegates. On the prayer card there is a suggestion which is so important that I repeat it here:

I intend to pray daily for the delegates of the United Nations and other world leaders that they may do God's will for all. I shall also pray for an awareness of God's presence in my own life so that I may understand and undertake my part in helping to create and maintain a peaceful world.

Imagine what would happen if ten million Christians were convinced that they should make a daily habit to pray for the delegates of the United Nations and for the President and for the rulers of Russia, and for those in authority in all other countries. If that happened I believe a miracle of reconciliation could take place all over the world. Indeed, I believe that a Pentecost would fall upon the churches because they were engaging in such a program.

Perhaps you agree that this is true. Here are three things that you, as an individual, can do in your own community to help:

1. Form the daily habit of praying for world leaders yourself, and of writing to them as you feel led.

2. Inspire your fellow church members to pray for the world leaders. Form prayer cells, or have people pray at the breakfast table with their families, or alone, as they prefer. They could have the prayer card by their bedside and pray before they go to sleep or when they awaken in the morn-

ing. It is well to have a tablet and a pen so that if you feel so led you can write and tell these world leaders that you have prayed for them.

3. Many churches are now dividing up the names of United Nations delegates among their church members, so that each delegate will be sure to get a special prayer from one or more members of that church. Then every delegate is sure to receive at least one letter from someone who is praying for him.

Let us calculate how many letters that could be. There are 100,000 American churches. If every American church wrote to each delegate in the United Nations, that would mean more letters than many of them have ever received on any subject in their whole lives!

The churches would begin to realize that in prayer they have the greatest power for good. Nothing stands in the way of such an experiment as this. I believe this country is more eager than it ever was before for such a prayer campaign. The low spiritual level of some churches may result in a small response to this challenge. Where that is the case, prayers for the United Nations and for our own government leaders would be the finest way imaginable to raise the level of those churches to a new high.

We Christians simply do not dream what power we have. We are committing a terrible sin against the world in failing to use it.

A very large and powerful section of the Christian Church has been neglecting to pray for our labor leaders and labor unions, yet labor has a power for the future of our country and of the world that is difficult to overestimate. We must pray that this power may be directed by the wisdom and love of God. Christian churches as a whole have ignored the people who lead the labor unions and the men who toil in our factories. Many Protestant churches have been guilty of seeking people who have financial resources and social standing, and of neglecting the workers, who do not have very much money. Our best Protestant leaders have unhappy consciences about this. Some church leaders are making a definite effort to befriend the labor unions and to prove that the church is their friend and is trying to help them.

We *must* include labor in our prayers. It is true that sometimes labor is as despotic as any dictator ever was. (For example, the longshoremen of New York held up the entire New York City and threatened it with starvation.) Many strikes seem unreasonable. Nevertheless, the labor unions have done a tremendous job in helping laboring people out of oppressive conditions; they have benefited the whole country when they have done that. We need to pray that they may get God's direction; that they may choose leaders who are deeply Christian; that the Church may influence them more and more, and that when they act, they may be God-led and not selfish.

Probably it is because I work among the lower three-fifths of the human race—the people who cannot read and write—that I feel a special urge to pray for them, as well as to help them. We must not neglect that part of society. Up to this time, alas, they have been the truly forgotten people. It wasn't that they were forgotten so much as it was that we never *knew* them. Include in your prayers, whether you are praying alone or in prayer groups, a prayer for the people who are trying to help the lower half of the world out of its misery.

Jesus told us to love our *enemies* and to pray for them. It is hard to love our enemies, probably even harder to love them than it is to pray for them. If we pray for them, it will be easier to love them.

But how can we pray for those with whom we are at

war? How can we pray loving prayers for the Communist leaders in Russia or in China? It is even difficult to pray for the candidate of the opposing political party! How can we pray for him except that he may lose the next election?

But we are not told to pray for people when it is *easy* to pray for them, nor to pray for them because we *approve* of them. We are praying for people because they *need* prayer, just as we feed hungry people because they need to be fed, or as we try to save a man's soul because his soul needs saving. We know that God wants us to pray for people who need prayer. That includes everybody. Paul says to Timothy, "God desires all men to be saved and to come to a knowledge of the truth," and "all men" includes the men in the Politbureau of Russia and the heads of the Chinese Communist party. He wants them to be saved, so if we pray for them at all we must pray for God's will for them—which is not their destruction but their salvation. And that *is* difficult!

But if we refuse to pray for our enemies, we have real reason to worry about ourselves. If there is anything clear in the teachings of Jesus, it is this: that as we treat others, as we think about others, so will God treat us. If we cannot pray for the salvation of our enemies, then the love of Christ is not in us, for Christ loved His enemies.

If we are to pray for our enemies, what shall we say? "Help us to defeat the Communists"? That is not enough. Shall we say: "Deliver us from our enemies"? That is not enough. Is it enough to say, "Save our enemies from the evil they are doing"? Yes, that is good, but I think even it is not enough. Is it enough to say, "Lord, give us peace"? That is good, but I think it is not good enough.

Here is what I believe would be enough to please God: "Lord, make all of us, both our friends and our enemies and ourselves, like Christ, so that we shall love one another."

That will do it. God is seeking a way to reveal Christ to the Communists. How can they ever see Jesus if they cannot see Jesus in us? And so, if we are sincere in our prayer, we not only pray that they may see the Lord Christ and follow Him, but that they may see the Lord Christ *in us* and in our action. We will pray that they may see the Lord Christ in the way our government acts.

We can never ask God for too much. Nothing is impossible to God. Usually we do not ask Him for enough. Peace is good, but to ask only for peace in the world would not be enough.

Our prayers go unanswered if we ask only to be cured on the surface, while the hidden evil lies deep down inside. God wants the deep decay removed from our world.

It is even harder to pray for our personal enemies than it is for our national enemies. Out of the depths comes the memory of an insult or an injustice that haunts us, and in spite of ourselves we find that we are resenting and disliking the one who wronged us. We try to drive that memory back into the subconscious. The psychiatrists say, "Bring it out—give it an antiseptic bath!" Prayer is the best antiseptic bath in the world. Indeed, it works when all else fails. If we bring our dislike out and hold it up in the presence of the Christ who forgave every enemy, it becomes cleansed, purified and burned out. So, when such an old resentment comes to mind, the one thing to do is to consider it as God's signal that the other person needs to be prayed for.

We should pray not only for those whom we like. We must pray especially for those whom we do *not* like. We pray especially for those who do not attract us.

The disciples asked of Jesus, "Teach us to pray." He gave them the Lord's Prayer. It is the perfect illustration of what we are trying to say in this chapter. It is a prayer for *others.* "Our Father" begins with the letter "O," and that "O" is as big as earth and heaven. Jesus tells us to ask that the Kingdom of God should come, and that His will be done in everybody on earth. When we pray, "Give us this day our daily bread," we are not praying for ourselves alone. "Our daily bread" begins with the letter "O," and that "O" means the entire world. There are two billion people for whom we pray when we ask for "our" bread.

If we use the Lord's Prayer as a formula, like a witch doctor trying to control an evil spirit, it is, of course, of small value. It is a superstition to think that we can memorize a formula, no matter how beautiful, and get any benefit out of it by repeating it without *thinking* about it. I suppose it does something to our subconscious minds, even if it is repeated in our sleep, but certainly it does not have the value that it would have if we thought about it, and if we felt it deeply.

When we pray for anybody—important or unimportant—how do we know what to ask? It is better, I think, to ask God's advice rather than to try to explain to Him what we want. The most important thing is not what we tell God about people, but what He tells us about them; not what we tell God to do but what He tells *us* to do. So here is a prayer which, I think, includes all that we can be sure is right.

Dear Lord, I pray for my friend James. Help him to pray, help him to ask Thee for Thy wisdom; help him to hear Thy still small voice; help him to do Thy will.

X

PRAYER IS A RADIO HOOKUP

In my book called *Prayer, The Mightiest Force in the World,* I presented the theory that the reason prayer for other people works is because it opens a channel—like the radio—between God and those other people. Our knowledge of telepathy is increasing; it now seems to be accepted by nearly all of the best psychologists and, I think, by most laymen as well. We have learned enough about it to know that our minds are, in some way, more or less tied together—part of the time, at least. The experiences of our lives convince us of this.

If you are like I am, you are often stunned to discover how well people know what you are thinking. I believe that we are related to other people, subconsciously, far more than we suspect. So our good thoughts of them help them. Even people who never *pray* for themselves have their minds reaching outward toward other people even if they do not reach upward toward God, and they are connected with us, more or less, on that subconscious level.

If we look up to God and think of Him and of another person at the same time, and say, "God, help him to want to pray," that thought may enter that other person's subconscious mind, which mind may send a message up to his conscious mind, saying, "You need to pray." He may look up to God and pray. In that instant you have built a bridge

115

of thought between him and God. We who do this habitually are convinced that it is a very potent power. The results are far above our expectations.

To make clear what I mean, we will suppose that we are praying for the President of the United States. We might use these words: "God, help the President in his great responsibilities to pray for Thy help. Help him to open his mind and to give Thee a chance to speak to him. May he hear and obey Thy will." If the subconscious mind of the President is reaching out to the people of the United States, seeking to carry out their wishes, he may receive in his subconscious mind that prayer which we have sent to him, and he may be reminded to look up to heaven and to ask God's help. The best person in the world forgets God part of the time. I have no doubt that the President of the United States, with his tremendous decisions to make one after another, forgets God a good deal of the time, and is helped by our prayer as he searches for an answer. If he looks to God, he gives God the chance to give him that answer.

I feel deeply about this matter of praying and holding others up to God because of the experience that I myself am having. A great many friends in America have promised to pray for our literacy program around the world. While we are on our tour, we are conscious that a hundred or more groups of these friends are gathering in various parts of the United States to pray, and that many of them are praying while they are at home, and I can feel a new fervor and a new courage in spite of difficulties at the moment when they are praying. And I think they make me want to look up to heaven and ask God for help. Days or weeks later I get a letter—"We were praying for you—did you feel it?" I can often reply, "Yes, and it made everything better."

When we pray for other people, we are not *persuading* God to help them. We do not change God's mind. We are *giving Him a chance* to help them. We become the channel for His will. We deliver His message by way of our prayer line, just as we would be delivering God's message if we sent them a telegram, or a letter, or telephoned to them, or went to talk to them face to face.

We might write to them; we might telephone to them, but instead of that, we can now send them a message by telepathy. Our minds are somewhat like an amateur radio set which both sends and receives messages, here, there, and everywhere. Prayer is an attempt to control or to use this for the benefit of our friends or for those who need prayer. Just as the weather and deliberate efforts to jam radio does obstruct those messages, so spiritual weather conditions and perhaps deliberate contrary thoughts may obstruct our prayers when we try to reach people. But if we persist, the spiritual weather will change and, sooner or later, we will "get our man" through prayer.

This suggests that we need not spend a long time praying for one person. My belief is that if we have a thought, or if we want someone to look to God, we reach him in a fraction of a second if we reach him at all. This means that we can pray for a great many people in the course of one day—for those we talk to, those we are looking at, those we read about in the newspapers, those we think about. The mind plays on hundreds or thousands of persons every day. Turn the thought into a prayer! Then if only one in a hundred receives the message which we send, we may bless two or twenty people. But my belief is that a large percentage of those whom we pray for do get our messages down in their subconscious minds, where every memory stays forever. I hope that we may one day prove that every prayer goes home and begins to work. A great deal of experimentation in this direction is needed, because there is so much we do not yet know, scientifically and exactly. But you and I do know enough to engage in this experimentation for ourselves. One wonderful thing about it is that we can do it anywhere, no matter what else we are doing.

Pause here for a moment and think of some man who needs prayer. During the busy hours of his day, he may be thronged with interferences; a thousand impressions— noises, voices, thoughts—may be crowding his mind. At that time our prayers may be crowded out of his mind. But if we pray for him when he is relaxed, then our prayer will reach him. He is not then too busy for a prayer call. It is at those very moments that he most welcomes prayer; he needs us most when he is asking a question. I believe that when people are puzzled, and ask themselves, "What shall I do about this?" they do receive our message when we say, "Look to God." And if they look to God, they get their answer.

So you who wonder what you can do for God and for the world have here at your fingertips the most marvelous power in the world. You may sit at home and "telegraph" all over the world the word that everybody needs most to hear: "Look to God. Ask Him for the answer." This is what I mean when I say that prayer is the mightiest force in the world. It is not only the mightiest unused force in the world, it is the most *convenient* to use. It is as available, every moment, as air. God is no respecter of persons. Nobody has more prayer opportunity than any one else. You can have access to the prayer microphone *at any time*. You don't have to pay a fortune for fifteen minutes of time! You are on a world-wide hookup the moment you want to be. You can be as powerful as you want to be if you get on the sending end of this radio. Stop envying those who are getting our radio messages across America today. You have a better way than they have, only you don't use it! You don't have to wait until the hour comes for you to send your broadcast. You can begin at any hour, anywhere, night or day. It is probable that the messages that we send at night, when people are asleep, are more effective than those which we send when they are awake. The power which we possess at this point and which we do not use is unbelievable.

What we know about the subconscious mind indicates that it immediately shuts out criticism. The subconscious mind shuts out criticism because it is afraid of criticism. So when you pray for people, do not pray *against* what they are doing; pray for what they ought to be doing. We help the things we think about and we help the things we pray about. I am afraid we help a cause even when we pray against it, or when we think against it. When we pray we are not like a psychoanalyst who is looking for trouble deep down in people's minds. We are like a sower who goes out to sow seed; we sow seed in the other man's mind in the form of ideas that we want to sprout and to grow in his subconscious and to affect his life.

When we pray for people we are sharing God's hopes and plans for them. *We visualize what ought to be.* We see it rising like a lovely palace out of their minds—out of what is, now. The idea is the blueprint which the mind works from. Every thought begins to exert a tiny pressure through every crack of that man's being. It begins to become true. First, thought, then reality. First, thought in us, then thought in the man for whom we pray. If we pray aright, our thoughts come from God; in one sense, it is God praying through us. Paul said that, so I am orthodox! He said we do not know how to pray as we ought, but the Spirit itself intercedes with words that cannot be uttered. It intercedes for us. So I believe that when we pray the "listening" kind of prayer, it is God who helps us to pray the right thing.

But criticism, even in a prayer, tends to kill, to block the subconscious. On the other hand prayer with a vision of something better gives life. It brings out and challenges the best in the other man. This is why, when we pray: "God, may Thy dreams for him come true," we become pipe lines to the man who needs our prayers.

It is true that people may deserve criticism, but we are not trying to give them what they deserve—we are trying to get them *saved* from what they deserve. The criticism they deserve will only do them harm. Only prayer will do them good. So here is a good rule: if we feel like condemning, *pray*. Such prayer begins to redeem him for whom we pray! There is no other way really to forgive one who has harmed you. There is no other way to stop him from being a harmful kind of person. Keep praying until the bitterness has melted away from your heart, until forgiving, redemptive love flows through you. Then it will redeem you as well as the other man. When we pray at the moment we feel like condemning, we make both ourselves and others better. Jesus said, "Judge not, that you be not judged." Judging kills, but prayer brings new life, if it is the prayer that aims at what the man ought to be and is not the hypocritical prayer of superiority, condemning the man for what he is. The devil tries hard to spoil our prayer with his venom—so when you pray, keep generous and sweet. Keep out the venom! That requires the grace of our Lord Jesus Christ.

The "soul power" of Mahatma Gandhi reminds us that if we follow the practice of praying for the best that others can become, we shall develop that mystical Gandhian soul power. It will slowly accumulate in us and become a power to sweeten and bless the world.

How much soul power can we accumulate? Nobody knows. Gandhi indicates that it is tremendous. He was able to influence, not only for his own lifetime, but *forever*, 350,-000,000 people in India and only God knows how many elsewhere. I confess that he is influencing me, even now. I think that the power we might accumulate is infinite, for the simple reason that God's resources are infinite. With Him nothing is impossible.

So, I repeat, let us not ask God for the "possible." Let us ask Him for as much as we believe He wants and let Him prove that it is not impossible. Whenever a thing is right but impossible, that is the time to pray! Jesus Christ never toned down His prayers, His thoughts or His deeds to other people's standards of the "possible." He did the impossible easily because He did what God desired. We don't have to compromise with the second bests—our poor second bests!— not if we know how to pray! What is troubling you? Leave it to God. It isn't impossible for Him.

Professor J. B. Rhine of Duke University, the famous parapsychologist, has now set about to prove scientifically that prayer is the greatest power in the world; he is appealing to men and women of all churches throughout the world who are known for their prayer lives to co-operate with him in this experiment. One of his most interesting and successful experiments thus far has been *making plants grow* by loving them and praying for them. Here you can have a carefully controlled experiment, and it does seem to be working a miracle. If it works on plants, it certainly ought to work on people! We needed Professor Rhine to invent prayer measurements for us. There is a difference between the experiments of a physicist or of a chemist and our experiments with prayer. The physicist can look on from the outside with his microscope while he tries to see what his experiment will do, but when we experiment with prayer we must try our experiment chiefly in the depths of our own souls. Others who look on from the outside may see diseases melt way, and they may see plants grow much more rapidly than ordinarily. But most of the experiment has to be tried in the secret chambers of our own hearts. That makes it more difficult to have scientific measurement of our heart-results. Even if we do see the result, we may not be able to determine why prayer worked for one man and did not work for another. Prayer cannot be weighed or measured or tested with a geiger counter. That is its disadvantage. There are always invisible intangibles beyond the reach of those "outside."

On the other hand, prayer has this great advantage—that anyone who is willing can test it for himself, anywhere. It doesn't require the observation of another man "on the outside." A man carries his laboratory within himself. It is his own soul, and he has it with him night and day. Moreover, a man can find human needs of every kind waiting for him on every side and he can try his prayer on those needs. A sincere Christian rapidly becomes an expert in this field. He does not need to go to a psychologist; in fact, a psychologist who is not a spiritual man can only do him harm. We can learn nothing from a man who knows less about the spiritual life than we ourselves know.

And it is not necessary to adopt some new theory, like Vedanta, or to become a Christian Scientist. You can be a thoroughly orthodox Christian. In fact, this experiment will make you orthodox, for it will verify the Bible; you can prove that the kind of prayer which Jesus practiced and taught works today as it did in His day. You can prove this without changing your theological opinions at all. You can prove it by fulfilling the conditions which He fulfilled. The most vital question in all the world today is whether what Jesus did, and what He taught, is possible for us, now.

For if Jesus was wrong, then everything is wrong. Then we have very little hope, except to face annihilation. If Jesus was right, then the only thing necessary is for us to become right.

We who are trying to prove to ourselves and to others what prayer will do, are more important than the scientists with their atomic theory. Thus far the atom has been used only to destroy. We would immediately save the atom and make it useful for mankind if we believed that Jesus told the truth. Men will mobilize all the energy in the world around useful programs for helping humanity if they can be induced to adopt the love of Jesus Christ.

If Jesus told the truth, then we Christians of today are living a lie even more than we are the truth; our lives are sixty per cent lie and forty per cent truth. All of us are caught in this lie, for our lives are denying His truth, even though we preach it with our tongues. And yet that Gospel must be proven true in our day. Where else shall we turn to save ourselves from the effect of the awful thing the physicists have let loose?

We who are Christians hold the world's fate in our hands, for whether the rest of the world learns the secret of Jesus or not depends on us. We cannot evade this; God challenges you and me to help our age push its spiritual knowledge beyond where it is at the moment. Our scientific knowledge is five hundred years ahead of our spiritual growth. I will not say of our spiritual *knowledge*; we have that, in words, in the Bible, but we do not have it yet in life.

We have this fearful responsibility. That is why we must pray for much more than for ourselves. The whole world is tied up with our prayers.

The greatest power comes from our prayer after we have overcome the temptation to hate a man and to hope for his harm. For example, if I pray for an enemy, when I am tempted rather to hate or to curse him, that prayer, I think, has the greatest power. We exert the greatest effort when we are overcoming an obstacle or lifting a weight. When we struggle, we are likely to feel more deeply, and where there is deep feeling, our prayer should have greater results, and I believe it has.

We need measurements for prayer. The geiger counter is employed to detect the presence of radioactivity. Litmus paper is used to detect alkali and acid. It is also possible for us to find a "counter" or a thermometer or a measure to tell whether our spiritual lives are effective. If we pray for the sick and they do not recover, I suppose that is some kind of a measure of our spiritual level. It would be easy to say that it is the will of God for them to remain ill, but that is putting the blame on God, and Jesus never did that. We have a verse from Jesus that perhaps we can use as a geiger counter: "If you abide in me and my words abide in you, you may ask what you will and it shall be done." Abiding in Him and keeping His words abiding in us means that we are in perfect harmony with Him, listening to Him, obeying Him, while we love other people and pray for them. He promises that if in all these ways we fulfil His conditions our prayer will be answered. And it must be that imperfection in us at some point that defeats our prayer. God is perfect, and we can never blame Him for an unanswered prayer. The uncertain quantity is myself. I am the one who usually does not fulfil all the conditions. If I had faith like the faith of Jesus and love like the love of Jesus and obedience like the obedience of Jesus, then I know that all disease would melt away when in His Name I commanded it to depart. So perhaps our inability to heal the sick indicates that we lack perfection in love or in faith.

It takes some humility and some courage to admit this, because if you are like I am your success in praying and securing help for sick people is not what you wish it were. It seems to rise and fall. But have you noticed that it rises and falls as your love for Christ and your faith in Him rise and fall? Have you noticed that it is at its best when your love is at its best and when your faith is most serene? I am not sure that it is fair to use this as a geiger counter or a measure of our faith. It seems as though some people have one gift and some have another. Indeed, Paul said this, and it may be that we are very strong in our prayer life in some other direction, while other persons are more effective in healing.

Jesus said that anybody could be healed if he had enough faith. In His home town, Nazareth, where they knew Him as a young boy and always thought of Him that way, He said their faith was weak and that it was because of their unbelief that He could effect no cures there. He said, "According to your faith be it unto you." If you want more proof there are scores of very good books packed full of marvelous evidences of answered prayer for anyone who wants to know the facts. Indeed, it seems as though we are coming into a new era. An ever increasing number of churches filled with radiant people are seeing healings, sometimes every day, sometimes every week. The medical profession also has gone a long way in psychosomatics, which reveals the effects of the mind on the body, either to make one sick or to make one well.

To a certain extent all of us know that this is true. All of us know that when we are in a distressed state of mind almost anything can happen—migraine headaches, for instance, and all kinds of ailments. This is so true that the point need not be labored. On the other hand, radiant faith, hope, and joy, love and fun are curatives. This we know. This is not new knowledge. But we have gone a great deal further than we ever did in the past in knowing this; we have gone so far in the past few years that nobody dare guess what the end may be. It is sometimes called "new medical knowledge," but, actually, it is merely agreeing with Jesus Christ, who knew it and said it two thousand years ago.

It seems likely that in a few years most medical colleges will have courses in the therapeutic value of prayer, just as they are now taking up psychosomatic study, and that faith will be a major concern in those courses. The doctors, though, may be running themselves out of business, for if our mental states are wholly right we should not have a fraction of the diseases we have now. Indeed, the American Medical Association now officially states that a great many more than half of our diseases are due to unhealthy states of mind. They used to say ten per cent. One wonders whether in another generation or two they will be saying ninety per cent. And so in this realm of health of mind and body we have a promising field for those who wish to help push forward the frontiers of deeper spiritual life, and it is one place where we can really see results.

A warning, though, is necessary. I believe that we ought to use all that modern medical science knows, adding prayer to that knowledge. God gave us everything we now know because He wanted us to use it. I think that Paul's statement about food, when he was writing to Timothy, applies in this matter of medicine; he said that everything for us to eat was given of God, and that we shouldn't hesitate to eat it. Of course, he meant everything that is *good* for us, and if medicines do us good we should not hesitate to use them. It is not a lack of faith but a lack of gratitude when we refuse to take what God offers. It is a great mistake to limit God and say "I will follow you in one way, but I will not follow you unless you follow my preconceived notions."

For those who desire to go further with this I suggest that they read *Recovery,* a book by Starr Daily, about the cures effected by Rev. Roland Brown, a former Baptist minister of Chicago who has seen miracle after miracle of healing through faith. I recommend that you read *The Healing*

Light, by Agnes Sanford, and *How to Find Health Through Prayer,* by Glenn Clark. I recommend that you read *Answer Without Ceasing,* by Margaret Lee Runbeck, and a little magazine called *Sharing,* published by Mrs. John Gaynor Banks of the San Diego Episcopal Church.

We all have a perfect right to try interesting experiments if they seem promising. It is not necessary to tell other people about those experiments until after they have been successful. For example, Mrs. Louise Eggleston, applying the knowledge that the subconscious mind can be reached during sleep when the conscious mind is not keeping it busy with sensations from the outer world, prays for people while they are asleep. She goes into a room alone and speaks aloud to the people or to God, repeating her message quietly, slowly, emphatically. She has had a long list of remarkable cures of diseases and of alcoholics, and she has brought reconciliation to broken families.

If you pray just before an interview with an important person on an important subject, you make doubly sure of its success. This is of course for two reasons. First, you prepare your own mind. Second, as I believe, you also prepare the mind of the person with whom you are going to talk. It is equally true that you will be more successful with a letter if you precede it with a prayer. If you happen to be a business man or a business woman with a secretary, it is a very good thing to make a practice of breathing a prayer over every bunch of letters you send out. Let your secretary share that prayer with you. Some of us pray for those to whom we are writing at the moment when we are signing our names, then the prayer gets there before the letter, and the letter which we are sending is the follow-up, which is more likely to finish what we already began.

If you agree with me that we are now discussing one of the most vital matters in the whole world, the discovery for ourselves and for others of the power of intercessory prayer, then you will want to establish contact with others who are more successful than you are. Dr. Glenn Clark of the Camps Farthest Out is seeking out those people, and through him their names and what they are doing can be ascertained. I happen to be a friend of many of these people, and I find that they are simply orthodox Christians, taking the Bible at its face value, believing that Jesus Christ is the Son of God, that He is living, and that He is keeping His promise to be with us always.

It is New Year's Day, 1954, in St. Luke's Hospital as I revise this chapter for the last time. I have made a New Year's resolution and have kept it for twelve hours! It is working miracles outside and glory inside my soul. It is a very simple resolution. I have resolved to say of everybody who enters my thought:

"Lord, I pray for ————," and so try to open the switch between him and God.

One nurse said, "It seems like Sunday today."

Another (not knowing me) said, "Did you ever think about entering the ministry?"

A third said, "They tell me you are a teacher. What do you teach—religion?"

And I had not said a word about religion!

Probably the *most important* proposal in this book for us is: Say of *everybody, everybody*:

"Lord, I pray for him."

XI

HOW TO BE A RIVER

In John 7:38, Jesus said, "He who believes in me, out of his heart shall flow rivers of living water." And again in John 4:14, He said, "Whoever drinks of the water that I shall give him will never thirst; the water that I shall give him shall become in him a spring of water welling up to eternal life." It is not by measure that He gives His spirit. He doesn't measure it out in a bushel basket. It flows in and flows out, like rivers—not even like one river. The way it operates reminds one of a huge river that flows into a delta: it flows in through one channel and flows out across the world in as many channels as there are people needing it.

This thought is also expressed by Paul when he says, "God's love has been poured into our hearts through the Holy Spirit." The chapter which precedes this helps us to realize how tremendous this concept can be.

There are three questions in connection with such a river. The first one is its source, and how much water is there to feed it? The second is: How big is the channel, and how wide is the valley through which it is to pour at the narrowest point? The third is: Where will it go? Is it free from dams and blockages so that it can flow out unimpeded?

Let us consider first the *source* of the river. The year

1949 was unusually dry in eastern United States, and our water supply in New York City was dangerously low. Everyone was warned to conserve water, and for some weeks men conserved it by observing a shaveless Friday. But wearing a beard was hardly the right answer to the water supply of New York. The permanent solution was far up in the mountains. It was to find and channel to New York a far greater water supply. In the Hudson and Delaware rivers there is enough for New York City and to spare, and if they ever went dry New York could tap the Great Lakes.

But the supply of the Holy Spirit is infinitely greater than this. It is as great as the heavens above us—but we are just like the people of New York: *we have to have our pipe lines reaching to the source.* So the Christian answer to a weak spiritual life and to religious ineffectiveness is a wider intake, not a smaller outflow. The entire world now waits for men and women who are large enough rivers of the Spirit to encircle the globe.

Keep the connection open! New York offers us another illustration here. One morning the *New York Times* ran big headlines: "Twelve Hour Black-Out in New York City!" The main connections were broken with the main city powerhouse, and all subways, street cars, etc. were halted. Millions of dollars were lost in one day. Here the largest city in the world had lost connection with its powerhouse. It is far more serious when the world itself blacks out and breaks connection with the Powerhouse. And that is what happens when people are out of contact with God.

Even if we spend a few hours or minutes a day with God, we do *something,* just as a turbine wheel does during that period. But it is only exercising a fraction of our total possibilities. If the connection is constant, then we are able to say with Paul, "I can do *all* things through Him who gives me strength."

We know now much more about bodily health than did people in the days of Jesus. When a body is weak, the germs which were always present and ready to attack multiply at our weakest point and may result in death. When the body lies dead, it is again attacked by millions of phagocytes, which were there all our lives but kept quite harmless while our tissues were alive. Indeed, this is so true that Jesus said, "If you are in full contact with God, not even a viper can harm you."

But the pipe line from heaven must also be wide open toward the world. It must have no blockages to prevent the free flow of the Holy Spirit. If all the blockages are gone and the channel is wide open to heaven like the wide-open mouth of the young robin which is fed by its mother, if it is wide open like an airplane sowing rice across a field in California, if it is wide open in the middle like the great current in the Mississippi, then the rivers of living water pour through us and they pour out across the world. Those rivers of living water carry everything with them. They sweep away obstructions; they break dams. They keep on rising to cover and to heal and bless the world. If a man can be wide open so that he himself no longer blocks God, then all the power and love of God's infinite heart can flow through and out in every direction. One sees a few such men and women who are uninhibited channels in every generation.

Some days there comes a sigh, a longing: "Oh, I wish I had more of God and more of Christ!" That is the key that throws the doors open for Him to enter our souls. If the longing is strong enough the doors fly open and we feel a Divine invasion. He enters when we feel like that, no matter whether we call Him "Christ" or "Father" or "Holy Spirit." He enters because we have invited Him in. Then we feel a quiet joy or a deep ecstasy.

I have just talked with a young woman this morning

who, after years of resisting God, threw her doors open. The disease which had plagued her for many years and which, I have no doubt, was the result of her resisting God, had disappeared. She was in such a state of ecstasy that she didn't want to eat her breakfast.

This young woman was afraid the new glow might leave her. She had reason for that fear. It would indeed leave her unless he began to give it away at once. I had to tell that released woman: "This new wonderful something must now be channeled into rivers flowing out to the world." She has fallen in love with her Lord, and now she must go with Him into His work in the world. For elation and peace and contentment are all good, but they are all only temporary. They are like the tingle of the wire when the electric current flows through, or like the vibrating of the pipe when rivers are rushing through. And they will stop unless the river goes on flowing. It is a wonderful experience while it lasts. This young woman felt that she had at last arrived, that this was what she was born for. She was having her second birth. It was to her soul what mutation is to plants and animals when suddenly a new variety or species appears far in advance of anything that had appeared before. When that entrance of God into her soul took place, it was the most precious thing that ever happened to her or that can ever happen to any human being.

If you have had this Divine love experience, you know what I am talking about without any further description. If you have not had it, no description will explain it. A man who is blind to red or blue can never be told what they look like. No words can explain it. He has to *experience* those colors to know. And so I realize that I am now talking only to those that have had the experience and do not need to have it explained. Nobody can explain it to those who have not had it.

We can't keep Him unless we give Him away. First, there is no room in our very little souls for so much of Him as He has to give. He has got to pour in and then pour out to others. Just as the rushing in of electricity demands that it shall pour on through, so it is with Christ.

Another reason we must give Him away, is that if we really have Him like this, it is the most important thing in the world for *other* people to share.

Many people's consciences plague them because they have not been doing their duty in telling other people about Jesus Christ. They are bothered because they are not soul savers. All of this becomes meaningless the moment you get an invasion like this dear girl experienced this morning. She won't be able to keep it back. She won't need to think about sharing it, because what is uppermost in her thoughts is the thing she will want to talk about. Out of the fullness of her heart her mouth will tell the story, her face will shine, and she will tell what her heart cannot contain. So, effectual witnessing is a matter of having something which it is impossible to conceal.

I started to write on a piece of paper this morning with my pen. But I couldn't make a mark; the pen was dry. It didn't matter how often I tried to shake or to coax the pen along. It had to be filled up. But then after it was filled up, it had to be used before I could put any more ink in it.

Just so, life is a balance of receiving and giving. But it is not rhythm. They both happen at once. And the peculiar thing about the Spirit is that it is inexhaustible. You get it by giving it, and the more you give, the more you get, provided your gates are open upward and open outward. You can't give it without getting it, and you can't get it without giving it.

The nearest analogy to this is knowledge. The man who tries to accumulate knowledge for his own sake as a rule gets bored to death by the process. He cannot remember it unless he keeps repeating it. But the moment he begins to share it with other people, if they are interested and receptive, it stays with him, and he enjoys it.

In my own business in working with languages I find that I must use the new words that I get, or I lose them in a very short time. The secret of learning a new language is to use it before you lose it! The same thing obtains in the spirit world. The law of that world is: "You get by giving, and you lose by failing to give." You lose when you stop giving, and you gain the moment you start giving.

This morning after an "All Night of Prayer" at the Camp Farthest Out people came to a number of us for a blessing. As I put my hands on their heads I asked myself, "Is this soul wide open for everything that God offers? Is she wide open toward *His community* and toward His world? Can God give her what He wants to give and flow through her to touch those who need?" And I seemed to sense that some of them were eager to be channels, while others, for some unknown reason, were blocking God. Being God's channel to bless others is a strange and wonderful experience. I at least had been richly blessed. And as I left that service, I said, "God, I myself henceforth will have one hand lifted toward the sky to let Thee pour in, and the other hand of my soul reaching out toward the world to let Thee pour on to them." It seemed to me this blessed morning that the only thing I needed to do in this world was to get started that right way every day.

I have never seen anything that quite illustrates what I mean so well as these lawn sprays that throw water on the grass in all directions as they go round. The water flows through and spreads out in a big circle to make everything grow. He that is open to God and men is like that: out of him flow, not drops of water, but *rivers of living water*.

The Holy Spirit is more like light than water. It isn't a liquid; it is an energy. One cannot write on this subject except when his own soul is vibrating and bursting with the joy of Christ's tingling presence. Or if he did write about it, it would be dead stuff. This water that we are talking about is the livest thing in the universe because it flows straight from the heart of God, straight through the heart of man, straight out to meet the need of the world.

The spiritual folk in many a frozen pew will call this "crackpot," but down in their hearts they know that it is true. I say this not as a rebuke, but in great sorrow, for they know not what they are missing. When Jesus was with His disciples, people said, "Why don't you fast and weep as other people do over your religion?" He answered, "The bridegroom is with them; they can't weep nor fast." What Jesus gave His disciples was radiant. And it was still radiant in the Early Church. The saddest thing that has happened to the Church of Christ is that it has lost its radiance.

I believe it is the universal experience that the things we desire in this earth are more or less disappointing when we get them. In addition, we always get something we hadn't expected. Suppose you inherit a million dollars. You have a headache with it because you are worried about where to invest it safely and worried as to how you are to keep away from people who want to steal or beg it from you. Your million dollars becomes your prison; it makes you afraid of the world. Or suppose you try drinking. Judging from the way some people behave, they get a tremendous temporary stimulus from liquor. But each day they have to take more and more liquor to get the same effect, and finally it becomes, as the Bible says, "a mocker" that ruins their lives.

But I am not referring now just to things that are

wrong. Take eating, for example. We get satisfaction out of food, but if we live to eat, we get less and less satisfaction from life. If we eat too much, we are soon plagued by a "bay window" and the fear of heart disease, and we are obsessed with the problem of how to slenderize without eating less. Our very pleasure becomes our master.

The athlete who lives for the fun of games faces the inevitable law of diminishing returns. His athletic life is short. The baseball player has to retire while still in his prime. He is soon incapacitated to compete with younger men. I do not know any exception to this rule in the world or in the realm of matter. But in the spiritual world it is exactly the opposite. The satisfactions may be small at the start, but they grow greater. It is as the song says, "sweeter as the years go by." Those saintly old men and women, with their radiant smiles, are reflecting a life experience which grew more beautiful every year. There is nothing to compare to the blessing and peace of one who has walked with Christ for a lifetime.

St. Augustine told us the reason for this. He said, speaking to God, "Thou hast made us for Thyself, and our souls are restless until they find their rest in Thee." There is a great vacuum in every soul. We try to fill it with all sorts of things on this earth, and they all fail. But when we turn to Christ and let Him fill it, He satisfies.

Our dissatisfactions are our growing pains. We are made to be unhappy with our present state because we are meant to grow into the sons of God. Without those dissatisfactions we would settle back in sleepy contentment long before we began to be the sons of God. So the Christian life is a strange combination of joy and discontent. We are happy to be on the way, but always longing to go further. We are satisfied, and yet we hunger and thirst. It will be that way all our lives, and it should be. We are like Paul, who said, "I have not already attained, but I press on toward the high mark to which I am called by Jesus Christ."

When Peter was preaching his great sermon at Pentecost, he was marvelously inspired. This uneducated fisherman who had his only schooling with Jesus Christ for three years, poured forth this wonderful vision: "Jesus, being ascended to the right hand of God and having received from the Father the promise of the Holy Spirit, has poured this out which you see and hear." That is what was happening at that Pentecost and it happens in every Pentecost.

The Father pours the Spirit out through Jesus, then through His disciples out to others and on and on through the world. On the first Pentecost day, the Spirit reached three thousand people.

So today you and I have only one responsibility. We must go forth with the flood gates wide open upward and wide open outward and let the rivers of living water flow from God to men. We must forget about ourselves. Our business is to keep open, and He will do the rest. We must forget about whether our words or acts are the best they might have been. All that is God's responsibility. Ours is to keep wide open upward and outward. God will come in; He will go through. He will reach the rest of the world through you.

Many people who are called geniuses feel that the music or the poetry or the vision does not come from them at all; it comes from *above* them, from *behind* them, gushing and rushing through like a stream of water bursting from a rock. Emerson said in his *Oversoul*: "From within or from behind, a Light shines through us upon things and makes us aware that we are nothing, but the Light is all. The little eating, sleeping, counting man we do not admire, but when the Light shines through him, then every knee bends."

Emerson was right, but he did not tell us the secret. He told us what we need—not how to get it. The secret is that the way to receive heaven and to let it pour through us is to be open above, in the center, and outward.

But just how do we keep open outward and upward? Is it a question of the will? Is it faith? Is it desperate effort? No, it is none of these things. The secret is in the great Commandment, "Love God and love your fellow men." It is easy to love God because He is lovable. But it is more difficult to love people. Indeed, much of the world is very unlovable, and yet that part of the world which is unlovable is the desert. There is where the land is bitter with alkali and dry and hard. And there is where we are to reach with the water of life.

So we are not to measure our love by other people's love, but rather the reverse. The less they are lovable, the more we should love them. If they don't love at all, we have to reach the whole way. We sing a simple little song in the Camp Farthest Out: "It's love, it's love, it's love that makes the world go round." Indeed, it is!

I still shudder at the memory of a municipal hospital I once visited. I went there full of eager expectations. At the door I was greeted with a hostile scowl. It gave me a sickening feeling. I wouldn't have been a patient in that hospital for a million dollars! One might better commit suicide some other way than breathe the poisoned atmosphere of that hospital. Until recently, most mental hospitals were fatal. The patient may have entered temporarily insane, but he was soon driven permanently insane. The attendants in these hospitals were mad, too, in every sense of the word. Love alone works in a medical hospital or a mental hospital or a pulpit or an office. There are just two alternatives that we face in this world—love or hell. For love is the absence of hell, and hell is the absence of love.

And so the living water is the water of love, and it expresses itself in our prayers, in our words, in our deeds. The more love you give, the more you have. The more love you give people, the more love they give back to you in return.

I suspect that some people reading these words will say, "I wish I could experience that condition, but I can't." And yet nothing is in your way except yourself. Do you the moment any situation arises instinctively ask, "What will I get out of this?" or "How does this person treat me?" If so, self is blocking that way. Try to cancel out every question about yourself. We keep blocking God by our sense of insecurity, and we are distressing God because we have that fear. Let Him sweep you out into the sea of His love. Forget yourself, your little self, in the glory of this larger Self. The self that reaches up to God and reaches around the world is the only real *You*. The little self isn't worth worrying about. A fine Camp Farthest Out song says this gloriously:

> Sweep over my soul,
> Sweep over my soul,
> Come, gracious Spirit,
> Sweep over my soul.
>
> Sweep out hate and fear,
> Sweep out hate and fear,
> Come, gracious Spirit,
> Sweep out hate and fear.
>
> Sweep in love and joy,
> Sweep in love and joy,
> Come, gracious Spirit,
> Sweep in love and joy.

Sweep over my soul,
Sweep over my soul,
Come, Holy Spirit,
Sweep over my soul.

The trouble with so many of us is that we strut and show off, trying to "make good" or to "be important," as are other people. We need, therefore, to become like little children, pretending to be nothing, and able to sing a little song as elementary as this:

This little light of mine,
I'm going to let it shine;
This little light of mine,
I'm going to let it shine,
Let it shine, let it shine!

Immanuel Kant, who is considered by many to be the world's greatest philosopher, laid down as a principle of life: "So live that if everybody else lived that way, it would bring the greatest good to the greatest number." We are sure that being a radiant channel for God is the best way for other people to live. We are sure it is the best way for us.

The tragedy of our world is that so few will open themselves at both ends so that the infinite abundance of God can pour down and out to meet the infinite need of the world. But we need not mope nor mourn over that tragedy. We can begin and discover that it doesn't take as many people as we thought to transform the world. When Divine yearning took hold of MacArthur when he was appointed to rebuild Japan, he worked a miracle. And I think that if we knew the truth underneath, we should see that it was the prayers of Kagawa that had reached through MacArthur to save Japan.

One of the most wonderful poems in the world is George Eliot's, *O May I Join the Choir Invisible.* It isn't as popular as it ought to be, perhaps, because it isn't popular in our day to be *invisible*. Perhaps you imagine you have to die before you can belong to that choir invisible? But you don't! It is a marvelous prayer for you and me here and now, as well as for those who are dead. I suggest that you read that little poem, in one sitting, before going on to the next chapter!

XII

GOD SPEAKS

THE MOST IMPORTANT DISCOVERY A HUMAN BEING EVER makes is that God can speak to him. When one makes this discovery it reorganizes his entire life. If he can hear God he can tap the source of all truth and all wisdom. God did speak to the characters in the Bible; that is the reason that we look on the Bible as an authority. All of us need to develop the spiritual ear that will enable us to hear God's voice. We also need to learn His language so that we will know what He is saying when we hear Him. He doesn't speak the English language all the time. He doesn't even use words all the time when He speaks to us. As a matter of fact, His vocabulary is quite large. He uses sights, sounds, smells, tastes, thoughts, beauty, sorrow, friends, indeed, every incident in life to speak to those who are able to understand His language.

And yet I have never found a book which tells you the language of God. You must learn it for yourself, just as an infant must learn how to use his own muscles by trial and error.

The Journal of the National Education Association, in December of 1945, printed a story about some children who learned to listen to God in a school in Massachusetts. Vera E. Smith, a lovely Christian teacher, was confronted by a very dull looking class. She determined to try the experiment of having them listen to God. She told them that "God is broadcasting all the time. Any boy or girl can pick up a message from God if he will put his receiving set in order. George Washington listened to God at a time of conflict; Abraham Lincoln listened at a time of crisis; I should like to begin with you this morning and have a listening period." Then all the children bowed their heads reverently and were absolutely quiet. After a few minutes Miss Smith asked the children if they wanted to say anything. There was no response. Two days later she tried it again with the children. She said, "When you want a program on the radio from a certain station, what do you do?" They responded, "Turn to the number of the station broadcasting that program." Miss Smith said, "In other words, you have to tune in your radio to receive that program. God is broadcasting all the time, and if we tune in to him we shall hear what he says. This morning, will each one of you turn on your radio and listen to God broadcasting? Everyone ready now, to turn on your radio!" They bowed their heads and closed their eyes. One child twisted his nose and another his ear, another his lip, as though he were turning on a real radio.

Then Miss Smith asked, "Who wishes to tell me what he heard?" Many hands were raised. One little boy, who had been doing very poor work in school, said, "God told me to work harder and get better marks." Another, who was in the giggling stage, said, "He told me not to be so silly." Another boy said, "God told me not to cheat when I correct my arithmetic papers." A girl said, "God told me that I should not whisper so much." Miss Smith says that the ability of the pupils improved until they were able to read six months earlier than the normal time required; one boy improved two years ahead of time. One of the children said, "We are an entirely different class from what we were last fall. Our minds are more alert and we are doing much better work in all of our lessons."

After several months the teacher asked the children what their parents thought, and one boy said, "My mother thinks that listening to God is a very good idea. She thinks that she will try it." Miss Smith says, "Toward the end of the year the pupils wrote a summary of what listening had done for them. They recognized what a slow class they had been when they entered the fifth grade and what a change had come in them both in their work at school and at home. So eager were they to let the other children in the school know what they were doing that they gave a play called "The Thinking Schoolroom," and presented it to the entire school of some five hundred pupils. In the audience were many parents and the school superintendent, all of whom made enthusiastic comments. One boy wrote enthusiastically of what had happened to him. He said, "Listening to God has made a change in me at school, at home and in my play. When I am home I do things more cheerfully. I used to whine and quarrel. At school I attend to my work better. I used to sit and daydream. At play I try to be a good sport. I have found that listening to God has made a great change in me."

Miss Smith also testifies what happened to her that year when she and her pupils were listening to God. This is what she says:

For several years I had been losing my earlier zest for teaching. It was becoming more and more a matter of routine. . . . Then came this new experience, and I found that not only the class but the teacher needed changing. God had several suggestions to make to me and I took them. Now my whole attitude is different. I am convinced that teaching is a most challenging opportunity. . . . I am finding that there is a power outside myself which gives me a plan for living . . . and gives me the strength, the wisdom, and the grace to live that plan.

Many of us wish we could have been in a school like that! But it is never too late to begin. Children learn every-

thing more quickly than do we who are older, but if we persevere we can learn too.

I suggest that we try listening to God *on the border
lines of sleep*. There are two such border lines: just before
we fall asleep at night or after we begin to awake in the
morning. At those times we are passive, and nearly free from
outside distractions and noises. Then God can speak to us
with His still, small voice. All you need to do in order to
start Him speaking is to fix your attention on Him, look up
at the ceiling where you lie, or close your eyes and say, "Lord,
speak, for I am listening." If your own noisy, feverish ideas
have subsided enough, there often begins to flow a gentle
train of ideas, fresh with the clean flavor of heaven. These
lovely ideas rise out of the deep unconscious. Many writers
have a pen and paper ready at their bedside to record their
inspirations before their treacherous memories lose what
comes to them.

This unconscious mind seems to have several windows
open. It is opened toward the *spirit world*, both the *good*
spirit world and the *bad*. It is open toward other minds. It is
also open toward our own conscious mind. But the conscious
mind can be the master of those windows, and it ought to be
master.

Hypnotism reveals how credulous and impressionable
the subconscious mind can be. Under favorable conditions,
every suggestion determines the direction the subconscious
will follow. It is pathetically gullible! The hypnotist can
make the unconscious mind entirely oblivious to pain. *Your
own conscious mind has the same control over your unconscious.* You can tell your subconscious mind whether it is to
be open to the voice of God or to the voice of the devil. Indeed, we are always doing this, even though we do not know
it. What havoc we play with God's growing wayward sons
when we open to the devil! Jesus might very well say of the

way we treat our unconscious minds, "Father, forgive them,
for they know not what they do."

If we are open toward heaven, we cannot tell *what* ideas
will flow into the unconscious mind. If we could do that the
ideas would not be fresh from heaven! There is always
the glory of surprise in messages from heaven.

To hear God we must do two things, not just one. The
first is to spend our days with our attention and our interest
fastened on things that are good. That is why Paul was
so wise when he said, "Whatsoever things are true, whatsoever things are honest, whatsoever things are just, whatsoever things are pure, whatsoever things are lovely, whatsoever things are of good report, if there be any virtue, if there
be any praise, *think on these things.*" For thinking much
upon these things plants seeds in the subconscious mind,
and opens the subconscious mind toward God.

The second thing we must do is to take time to listen
to those voices which come up from the subconscious.

Our minds are beaten and wounded by the pitiless
sounds and sights that crowd in from the outside world. We
are defeated, terribly defeated by our own world. The radio,
the noises that swirl about us, our social engagements, our
work, all crowd out our own thinking, crowd out any chance
of listening to our own deeper, subconscious mind. That is
why the Quakers are very wise when they go to their meet-
inghouses and sit in complete silence for an hour every week.
Moral Rearmament varies this by listening in silence with
pencil in hand.

It is difficult to become calm and receptive to God. But
the more difficult it is, the more necessary it is for us to discipline ourselves. If our minds refuse to become still it may
prove that "the cares of this world and the deceitfulness of
riches are choking the word."

The pursuit of riches chokes the word just as much as

their possession. We must not expect that we can turn from a day of crass materialism, where we were seeking advantages for ourselves, and expect thoughts to flow freely from heaven into our feverish brains. The occupation of the day cannot contradict what God tells us at night; we cannot live double lives. Many a business man, if he reads this paragraph, will feel like hurling this book out of the window in desperation. He knows that he has *got* to think about his business; in other words, he must be materialistic during the day. Therefore he will conclude that listening to God is not for him!

But there is a better way: *That is to take listening to God into his business.* He can secretly commune with God all day. To hear God properly requires the whole day, not just five minutes early in the morning.

Genius in any field is rightly called "the power of intense, continuous concentration." This is as true of genius in religion as it is true in art and science. Our minds work all day in deciding what we should ask for, and what we should get. We do not "create" our ideas. They come from somewhere—up from memory or from other minds or from God, or possibly from the evil spirits in the air, as Paul said. Our thoughts do not *originate* with us. There are two entrances to the mind, and we allow thoughts to come in by one or the other of those two entrances. They come down through the conscious mind, which acts as a guard, or they come straight through the ether from other minds, or straight from God. If ideas come to our conscious mind from other people, we accept or reject them according as we find them palatable or not. The subconscious mind tries to take the impressions it receives through the conscious mind or directly through the ether, and make them orderly, for the subconscious mind wants everything to be reasonable. This is why we can solve mathematical problems in our sleep if we have given enough attention to those problems in our waking hours. We give them to the unconscious mind and that mind goes to work on them during the night. It is in this attempt of the subconscious to organize all the facts into a reasonable whole that makes us create.

Hearing God speak is, as we have said in a previous chapter, not a matter for a few minutes but a matter for all day every day. We shall grow better and better at it. We must look for God and listen for God in every transaction and pleasure and problem of the whole day.

A few years ago it dawned on me that the language of God is infinitely greater than all the words of all the languages in the world put together. The large dictionaries have about six hundred thousand English words; it is said that the Oxford unexpurgated dictionary has three million English words. But the vocabulary of God is far greater than that! He uses all the words of every language, and yet most of His language is not spoken words at all. It is written into His universe for those who can read. For example, when one takes a walk alone God speaks from every direction to those who can hear and those who can see. William Cullen Bryant in his *Thanatopsis* said it this way:

> To him who in the love of Nature holds
> Communion with her visible forms, she speaks
> A various language; for his gayer hours
> She has a voice of gladness, and a smile
> And eloquence of beauty, and she glides
> Into his darker musings, with a mild
> And healing sympathy, that steals away
> Their sharpness, ere he is aware. . . .

Twenty years ago on the island of Mindanao in the Philippines, the high-school students in our church began to write a dictionary of God's language. They never finished it—indeed, nobody ever will finish it. The world would hardly contain the volumes such an unexpurgated dictionary would fill. For the very universe is God's language. "The heavens declare the glory of God and the earth revealeth His handiwork."

These high-school students began by taking the words in Webster's dictionary, trying to imagine what God is saying through each word. They found it to be a most fascinatting game. I too was fascinated when I saw how fertile was the imagination of these young people. They would take a walk through the fields and forests, or out under the night sky, and ask what each thing that met their eye or ear said about God. What does a tree say about God? What is God saying through the flowers? What is He saying through the quiet sky? What is He saying through the people we meet? What is He saying through the ground on which we walk? What is He saying through the birds who fly over our heads? Maltbie D. Babcock sang:

> In the rustling grass I hear Him pass,
> He speaks to me everywhere.

If one walks with God as Maltbie Babcock did, one will discover that God is indeed talking to us every instant we are awake, and probably even when we are asleep. One will discover that the divine plan that Glenn Clark talks about is not mere poetry, but the deepest of all truths. God is encompassing you and me and everybody every instant with His best training for sonship. A deeper insight would reveal that He cares for every human being, not only for *some* of us but for *all* of us; not only in some countries, but in all countries; not only for the literate but for illiterate; not only for some colors but for every color; not only for those of one religion but of every religion. We would see the whole human race marching toward "that far off divine event toward which the whole creation moves."

I realize that this statement is a venture of faith. It appears to fly directly against the evidence of one's eyes, especially among the lower three-fourths of the human race among whom I work. Everything that happens to everybody is certainly not good. Much if not most is wicked. This is the testimony of our eyes and of the Bible. And yet, what is wicked in the world is not what God does or what He neglects to do; it is what man does. Even when the courts call an accident "an act of God," it is often true that someone in that accident had deliberately or recklessly placed himself where that accident could take place.

I have just been reading the thrilling book called *Annapurna*, by Maurice Herzog, about how the frost froze off the fingers and toes of the men who climbed to the top of the mountain. Nature did that, and yet these men put themselves where nature would do it, and they expected to be treated roughly. The spiritual experience which came to Herzog, he would testify, justified his agony a million times.

I think in the next life God will gather up the sufferings of the whole human race for the blessing of them all. I think this universe had to be "made perfect through suffering." Physical pain has been the watchdog protecting life, pushing life higher. Somebody should write a book on "The Values of Pain." Mental suffering is in most cases a part of our spiritual "growing pains." When the present seems intolerable and we reach for that which we have not yet attained, we are struggling in the travail of childbirth toward something which God is still creating. As Paul puts it, the whole world is in the pains of childbirth bringing forth the sons of God.

We complain constantly about our suffering, as though it were our worst enemy. Though we would not dare to say it, we *feel* like saying that God deserves our censure for that! But I think if we understood everything we would realize that pain is always remedial, physically or spiritually.

Without pain children would burn off their fingers, or cut them off. Man is forever beginning to destroy his eyes, his stomach, his feet, until pain comes and stops him. If God can be criticized at all on the score of pain, He could be criticized because, in some cases, He doesn't send it *soon* enough. I cannot think of a single instance where pain came too soon.

The trouble with cancer is that it does not hurt soon enough. If it did hurt badly enough and soon enough, we should have it treated or cut out in time. You may ask me, Why does it hurt at all, then, if it is too late? Frankly, I don't know. I think that the chief riddle of pain is that it often comes too late.

But I do know what cancer has done to many people. I know a woman who never had the slightest use for religion until she spent months of pain with cancer, and then she began to have wonderful experiences with Christ. As she was about to die she cried in glory, "Oh, I see heaven, and Jesus there waiting for me." She died with the smile of a saint. It looks as though that cancer had saved her soul. She had been made perfect through suffering. So, when we cannot see the physical reason for suffering, the spiritual purpose in the mind of God is often, though not always, clear. It is often pushing us from behind like the stubborn donkeys that we are.

Of course, it is obvious that that does not explain all pain. I am sure we do not know enough to explain all pain, but it does *justify* most of it.

You probably know that it has protected you and often pushed you higher. As for me, I must confess that I have made my greatest spiritual growth in those weeks and months when I was suffering the most with social or mental or spiritual pain.

I believe that when we face God on the Last Day we

shall praise Him not for the ice cream and cake we enjoyed on this earth but for the spiritual growth which came in pain and anguish. That is eternal.

> And from the ground there blossoms red
> Life that shall endless be.

God has infinite variety at His command. This may be seen in any bush or book. But those of us who seek Him directly in prayer find that same riot of variety. This is the reason why the witness of the saints seems so conflicting. God comes to each of us in ways never predictable. This is one of the things that the sticklers for orthodoxy overlook— that just because God came to one man in a certain way is no evidence at all that He will come to everybody else in the same way. I think He may come to people in about as many ways as there are people, just because God abhors monotony and loves variety. Don't listen to those stuffy little men who not only try to cramp other people but to cramp as well their own capacity to experience God. God wants to come to them with surprises, but they reject surprises because they are not found on "the approved list." They try to whittle God down to their own finite image. All they do is shut out God; as Emerson said, "The exclusive in religion exclude only themselves."

Those who think God must obey man's scientific laws are just as stuffy in the realm of science. The true scientist and the true saint walk in humility, admitting that they know little, and are eager to discover new truth. When God breaks through He plays havoc with our little rituals and restrictions.

One night not long ago I was sleepless. I saw a long room, in the center of which sat God with Christ beside Him. It wasn't necessary for me to examine whether this was orthodox or whether it was a picture out of Revelation or Ezekiel.

It was God coming to me in one of His fresh ways. All I needed was to believe and to be glad. The Lord Jesus Christ and I spent hours in conversation; I no longer remember it all, but bits of it come back to me. Jesus said:

Here is where the Father and I spend our time in secret interviews. I ask the Father about everything before I say it or do it or even think it. And so now when I speak the Father speaks just as much as I do. My deed is His and His is mine, since I forever and forever obey Him.

"The Father and I have invited you to come in and have your secret interview with us tonight, here in this long room. It is the perfect time, for there is no other sound or sight to distract you. In this world of the Spirit it is not rough and crude and loud, as it is in the material world. Compared to those noises you hear all day outside, our voices are very still and very gentle. The Father and I want you to learn to obey constantly, just as I do. Before you can do that you must learn to hear, because if you cannot hear you cannot obey. So tonight you are taking a long stride toward becoming a full-grown son of God. To be fully grown means only to spend your life, day and night, with the door wide open into the secret audience room with us.

Your best thoughts have been flowing from us, the thoughts which had power to transform other people. In those fleeting moments when you whispered for help you opened the door to this audience room and we could give our instant answer.

Tonight the Father and I are helping you with a clearer vision of our secret interview chamber, so that you may glance up into it at every moment when you are hesitating and get our perfect answer. This room is in the front of your head, although it extends out wide beyond your own body. When you wish to consult us, lift your eyes a little and there we are.

Your game with minutes was in the right direction, but tonight you are going to step beyond that game into the game with moments. One of the songs which best express the goal for you all in your world is:

> "Moment by moment
> I'm lost in His love.
> Moment by moment
> I've power from above."

That word 'above' is not beyond the stars but just over your own eyes. In the secret audience chamber, where the Father and I want to meet you moment by moment and enrich you from our limitless variety, fear will go when you learn to look up, even when the world swirls about you, for the Father and I are ruling the universe. Life experiences will test your faith, but they will never harm you.

Not only is God speaking to us every moment and everywhere, but He is also doing everything He can to help us. In Romans 8:28 St. Paul says, "We know that in everything God works for good for those who love him." And I think Paul might have ended his sentence more quickly, "In everything God works with *good*," not only in those who love Him but ultimately in those who do not. If they are not following His will He works to bring them back to follow His will, and if that involves suffering on their part so that they will turn away from wrong, that will prove to be a benediction to them also. To say that God always does good and never does bad is an understatement. *He always does all the good that needs to be done.*

If we could get hold of that truth clearly, all fear would be taken out of our hearts. "If God be for us, who can be against us?" That means *us.*

But, you might add, does this not paralyze our passion for right? If everything is as right as the Christian Scientists believe, why try to improve anything or anybody? I think the answer to that is easy. Sufferings of all kinds are real, and they reveal a real injury or disease or danger to be removed. Pains should stir us to compassionate service like that which we see in Jesus. Suffering is not what God wants in the world. He uses suffering only to help us to what He *does* want, which is to bring His children back to Him and to help them grow. Men are not right. Suffering reveals that men are not right. God is always right, but men are mostly wrong. The things which cause us to cringe and to weep in the world are symptoms of the deep wrong which is in men themselves.

I realize that it is impossible to throw the blame for all the suffering of the world on the wickedness of men. Can we blame the savagery of lions and rattlesnakes and sharks or dinosaurs on the wickedness of men? They were here long before men came on the scene. You can say that ninety-nine per cent of the world's pain occurs without any man knowing it. But we do not know how much pain there is when a lion breaks the neck of a zebra or a big fish swallows a small one. Is there any? All I am saying is that we do not know how much needless suffering goes on in the jungle or the sea.

Sin is very deep. Curing surface troubles like *hunger* and *disease* is not curing the deep, hidden trouble; it is only curing the symptoms. God is unsatisfied until the worst of all diseases is cured. That disease is separation from God. When we get back into God so that His Spirit has a perfect channel through us we have abounding health of soul and body.

We are prodigals. We arrive home only when we learn to live every second with our heads pressed up against the breast of God whispering, "Father, what next? What shall you and I together think, say, write, hear, see, and do? What next?"

Perhaps one should not say, "What next?" but "Who next?" for it is persons that really count with God. Things do not count at all, except as they help or harm people. And so at last we would be saying most of all, "Father, *who next?* For whom shall I pray? Of whom shall we think together, to whom shall we listen or speak or write, whom shall we help, to whom shall we bear witness, whom shall we praise and love and guide? Father who next?"

Asking that question in all its infinite varieties all our waking hours and hearing His answer would be the perfect life which Jesus lived and asks us to live. We would be asking it not only when beginning or finishing a task but all the time that we were performing our tasks, just as Brother Lawrence did while he wiped his dishes. It would become more than a habit, it would become an invariable way of life, and at last it would become involuntary.

We must not understate its difficulty. It is as exacting as learning to become a master on the piano. I suppose it is easier for some people than for others, but it is an arduous road for everybody. It is not as arduous, however, as the way of the transgressor, for every step of this way toward Christ is a joy and a glory. At its highest it means that instead of thinking alone you listen to God; *you think by listening to Him.* Instead of talking to ourselves (as we do if we have not learned this new art), we talk to God in an endless, quiet fellowship, never hurried, never worried, never tense, but always aspiring for a somewhat closer walk with Him. For the goal which is the fullness of the stature of Christ is far beyond our sight. Like Longfellow's youth in Switzerland, we are forever saying, "Excelsior!"

The attainment of constant communion seems to be high and hard to those of us who have not yet attained it. We are still spiritual children all the weeks and months and years that follow our first resolves to follow Christ. I suppose only those who have gone up ahead of us on that high road hand in hand with God can ever know what it is like. There are no words to express the experience, so those who have never been on that highway can understand it. It needs a vocabulary of its own, and when that vocabulary is spoken nobody but saints in heaven understand it. To try to transcribe it into man's speech has been difficult for all the prophets of all ages. They were trying to describe in words that did not exist that which others never even glimpse. But this much I believe we all can understand. One can ask God questions and hear God's answers. Sometimes that conversation is aloud, sometimes it is silent. We need no carefully thought-out questions; we need only to wait. As the Psalmist says,

> Wait thou for God,
> Wait patiently for Him.

Wait, listening for him to speak. Do not crowd God; do not wait in eager impatience, but in patience, to hear Him and to do what He tells you to do. It is impossible to record what comes to you, just as it would be to record all the thoughts that crowd into the mind in a day. God talks just as fast and just as naturally as we think.

We who have tried both ways of thinking—one with and the other without sharing it with God—know that there is as much difference in the two levels of mind as there is between heaven and hell. Without communion of this kind with God, the mind runs along much like a popular weekly magazine, if indeed it does not even sink below that low level! But when one is *en rapport* with God, listening and answering, then one's thoughts are wide and pure and selfless and creative. It is the difference between the worm in the ground and the airplane soaring thirty thousand feet above the ground. The worm sees a few inches ahead; the other sees far around on every side and into the future. The worm is interested in himself and the seer is interested in the whole world. And the soul in constant contact with God is far more than thirty thousand feet high. He is God's bridge from heaven to earth. He is like a tall tree with its head in the clouds and its roots in the soil. Through that soul God walks among human beings as He did in and with Jesus.

There is a warning needed, however, at this point. We must forever be on our guard against cocksureness that what we heard was really the voice of God. We have a very subtle and dangerous tendency to mix His pure message with wishful thinking. We instinctively hope that God will talk to us about ourselves. We pander to our desire for comfort or enjoyment, or flattery, and unless we understand our mental processes we are likely to expect only messages that please us and only messages about ourselves. You have read all through the pages of this book that God is forever seeking to carry us *past ourselves*. We, on the other hand, are forever seeking to drag God down to ourselves. The contest goes on between us and God all day every day. It is a war between the *little* life which we inherited from the millions of years that have gone before us and that larger life to which we are called in the eternity that lies ahead of us. We are going to find the larger life by losing the little life—the little life which seeks self. God calls us to pour ourselves into world need. He asks us, when need be, to lose our physical lives in that.

We are therefore able, as Paul says, to "test the spirits." When we receive messages from some secret source, we have a measuring stick to test whether those messages come from below or from above. The messages from below pander to our little selves; the messages from above call us out of our little selves to a larger self. This needs to be said very, very often! Even among Christian people there is a sanctified selfishness that differs from other kinds of selfishness only in that the satisfactions which it seeks to achieve are "spiritual." He who struggles *only* to save his own soul does not get that message from God. If he does not want to carry other souls with him he has not yet touched God.

There is a very widespread religiosity which begins and ends with self. Men belong to church for what they can get out of it for themselves here, and perhaps they look upon it as a sacred life insurance policy for a possible future life. This is the devil's counterfeit. This is not the religion of Jesus Christ. Our religion does not even begin to be Christlike until we reach out to save the whole world.

So, if you wish to test the voice of God, ask yourself whether your thoughts reach beyond yourself to help other people.

John learned from Jesus to declare: "God is love." Love does not mean self-love. John also says, "Beloved, if God so loved us, we ought also to love one another." That is the authentic word of God. John says again, "We love Him because He first loved us." That is authentic. It reaches outward. John says again, "He who does not love does not know God." That is authentic. It reaches outward. He says, "Let us not love in word or in speech but in deed and in truth." That sounds like the voice of God because it reaches outward. John says again, "This is the message that we have heard from the beginning, that we should love one another." That sounds like the voice of God. Again John says, "If we love one another, God abides in us and His love is perfect in us." That is the voice of God. It reaches outward. John says again, "If a man says I love God and hates his brother, he is a liar. For he who does not love his brother whom he has seen cannot love God whom he has not seen." That is the way God talks.

The spiritualists insist that the earthbound spirits are trying to invade our minds constantly. Maybe they are. One does not need to believe that if he does not like it. But one thing on which everybody does agree is that very "earthbound" *ideas* keep invading the mind all the time, and to discriminate between those and the ideas of God is far from simple.

One ought not only to read the Sermon on the Mount

over and over and over, but he also ought to memorize every word of it. For example, if the impulse comes to *judge* somebody else, to *criticize* or *punish* or *hate* or *defeat* or to *surpass* another person, it is very human, but it *does not come from God.* It will not stand the test beside the criterion of "God is love." It is wholly contrary to what Jesus said, "Judge not, that ye be not judged. . . . *Love* your enemy, do good to those who hate you, pray for those who despitefully treat you." Anything that is contrary to that does not come down from God.

God speaks when love speaks.

What love can do God can do.

Where love is God is.

But even that alone is not safe. For the word "love" is one of the most vague and ambiguous words in the whole English language. It is more ambiguous than it is in the ancient Greek in which there were two words, *agape* and *eros.* Our English word "love" covers romantic love, the love of material things, and the "love" of St. John. The love which is God is love with the picture of Christ in the center.

We have been talking about how God speaks. We need also to ask ourselves, "How do we hear?" How do we use that key that opens the floodgates heavenward? We do it in prayer, and it is much simpler than we usually think. It does not require some erudite supermind like that of Gerald Heard to tell us how to do it. A little old woman in a rocking chair, if she knows her Lord, can understand it just as well as some spiritual or intellectual giant. We need not strain, we need not use exactly the right words, we need not put our bodies in the right posture. Indeed, paying much attention to form deadens our ear to God. All we need is faith. We *believe,* then we simply say to the Unseen whom we expect to be near us and to answer us, "Lord, what have you to say to me?" And He answers. At first His answer may not be very clear. That is because we are not yet familiar with God's voice and do not know whether it is God speaking. When God spoke to the boy Samuel he thought it was Eli speaking! The great mistake we make is to give up too soon. It is the experience of the saints that they often have to wait an hour or two before they are sure that they hear God. "Take time to be holy," applies when we are trying to hear God. Remember, He is in you. Or, if you prefer, the Holy Spirit is in you, and you and He are listening to the Father.

Jesus said, "Without me you can do nothing." He might well have said, "Without me you can think nothing, and without me you can hear nothing." Unless we open our ears and eyes to God, and go hand in hand with Jesus, we shall neither think anything nor say anything worth saying or thinking.

It is a misfortune to be too brilliant. Some people think such brilliant nothingness that they never feel the need of Jesus. Lucky is the man whose brain stands still unless he prays!

XIII

HOW WE CAN HELP GOD

IF OUR HOMES AND OUR EDUCATION WERE RIGHT, EVERY young American would ask before choosing his life work, "Where am I needed most, and what is the best way in which I can help the world?" The influence of the church and of my home was so strong in my own life that I did ask that question; for me the answer was, "Go to Mindanao, Philippines, as a missionary."

But where I was needed most was far from easy. In disappointment and distress I was driven back to God until I was close enough to Him to learn how to be directed by His will. This happened on Signal Hill, Lanao, Philippines.

Alas, I have vacillated since then between the God-directed hours and the hours in which I forgot God or even refused to hear Him. Now I know by long, often bitter, experience what happens to me when I neglect or refuse to let God lead. Without God every plan fails.

When I keep saying to God, "I want to do your will," and I keep listening and saying yes to Him, then everything comes out right. If I forget about God and begin to think again that I can go it alone, things go wrong. If I remember Him and try to keep following His will, and whisper to Him, "What next, Father?" just trying to follow, then He opens doors. I believe He does that for everybody. In other words,

162

163

we must look toward God, listening and saying yes, and then toward others' needs and saying yes to their needs.

If I were a young man again I would choose my career where the world needs me most. There is an idealism in youth which rises to the challenge of need. Every college should have a good course in geography taught from the point of view of world need; then college students could find out where they are going to fit in by studying this world need. Our unfortunate sectarianism prevents schools and colleges from teaching young people what they most need to know. The young man needs to learn the importance of being God's channel, until it is as natural to him as breathing.

Everybody realizes that at times we are definitely helping God, but few realize how much God depends on us to help Him. Many people help God without ever thinking about Him. The Bible says that God used Cyrus, the ancient Babylonian king, although Cyrus knew nothing of God. God is using the Communists today to make us examine ourselves and see whether we deserve the friendship of the world. We are working harder to help the world because of their threat, yet they deny that there is a God.

At the Camp Farthest Out, Forrest Musser made a picture of Christ. One hand is lifted up toward the sky; the other hand is reaching down toward needy people at his feet. That is perfect; just as Christ becomes God's bridge to lost humanity, we at our best become God's bridge in the same way. We let Him use our hands and bodies to achieve His purposes.

Children's poetry so often reveals the profoundest truth. Here, for example, is a poem that the children know, but the older people usually have forgotten:

> He has no hands but my hands
> To do His work today.
> He has no feet but our feet

To lead men on His way.
He has no tongue but our tongue
To tell men how He died.
He has no help but our help
To bring them to His side.

Two verses in the 9th and 10th chapters of Mark are richer in meaning than appears at first glance. When Jesus was coming down the mountain from His transfiguration, He found at the foot of the mountain the disciples whom He had left behind, and a boy with an epileptic fit. The father of the boy said to Jesus, "If you can do anything for my boy, have pity on us." And Jesus answered, "Did you say: 'If you can'? All things are possible to him who believes." Then He cured the boy. The disciples asked Jesus why *they* had failed to cure the boy, and He said, "This kind can not be driven out by anything but prayer and fasting."

Those disciples *had* been praying. What, then, did He mean? He meant, "Let your whole time be dedicated to prayer." The capacity to channel enough of the power of God to cure that boy had to grow and grow day by day as people prayed and allowed God to make their pipe lines bigger. Some things can be driven out by nothing but perhaps years of prayer. If, therefore, we fail to accomplish something difficult, like curing an epileptic, here is our straight answer: We need to devote more time to prayer to God in order to help Him do the hard things.

In the 10th chapter of Mark Jesus was talking about rich people. He said, "It is easier for a camel to go through the eye of the needle than for a rich man to go into the kingdom of heaven." That sounded impossible. The disciples asked in amazement, "Who then can be saved?" And Jesus replied—these are words we must memorize—"With men it is impossible, but not with God. *All things are possible with God.*"

They are possible *with God,* but not for us alone. When we try for a little while a day to become channels of God we are unable to see much result. The reason is obvious, so obvious that perhaps we miss it. If a boy saw a champion weight-lifter lifting a four-hundred-pound dumbbell, and the boy tried to lift it and failed, he would hardly be silly enough to say, "If he could do it, why can't I?" That champion weight-lifter had been in training for years.

Examine that sentence again: "All things are possible *with* God." It doesn't say, "All things are possible *for* God." It means that God exerts more power when you work with Him. Jesus may have implied, *"when* you help God." The scripture does not make it clear whether the word "with" means "if you are with God," or whether we can read it, "All things are possible if you and God *work together.*" Evidently God is not doing all things that need to be done in the world by Himself. *Could* He if He wanted to? Everybody asks that question; nobody has ever answered it. All we know is that He doesn't. But may I venture a guess at the answer? I think that He has made the world so that He needs us, so that while helping Him we can become His co-operating sons. I think that is it, although there may be a deeper reason than any of us can fathom. At any rate, all we know is that God waits until we help Him.

A vast number of people are kept from Christ because they cannot throw off their past. But that is what the cross means. Jesus on the cross threw off our past. The past doesn't prevent Him from using us in the present. When Zaccheus the tax gatherer followed Jesus his past was wiped out. So was the past of Mary Magdalene. That is the greatest glory of the cross for us. It crossed out our past. If we turn and let God have the present, He can make the present and the future victorious.

This needs to be said because so many people are defeated by their past. They are afraid to face God because of their past and, therefore, they are useless in the present.

Thank God, what I have just said of a man is also true of a nation and of the world. Civilization has had a very ugly past. We had just better not try to defend it! Our Western civilization has been living the way that leads to destruction. It is all the more ugly because we have so often talked in a sanctimonious manner about being a "Christian civilization." We have been like the devil wearing the mask of Christ. But if we turn, and repent, and begin to help the world in the spirit of Jesus, it is astounding how quickly things will change. In my own experience around the world I have seen how many nations have been changed from hate to love. It can be done in a year if we go at it seriously.

In 1899 the Philippines hated America. Within a few months Shurman, who was sent out to explain our motives to Aguinaldo, had made the Filipinos our friends. At the end of World War II Japan was our enemy, but within a few months General MacArthur had changed that nation to a friend. Germany was our enemy at the end of World War II, but today Western Germany at least is our friend. Who has not seen hate turned to love in nations as well as in individuals? If we continue an unselfish effort to help mankind wherever mankind is in need, we shall find that hate slinks back into hell and that love will take its place all over the world.

Is God, then, defeated until we work with Him? A part of that answer is so easy that it seems ridiculous even to mention it. You can't defeat God or enslave Him. All of us might be defeated, but He will survive. In His vast universe the defeat of the human race is but the failure of a tiny little speck in space. God can do all this again if He wishes. A thousand years with Him are as a day. So we can say that He is delayed, and that He will wait. God has been thought of as "playing a chess game" with the universe, and with no time limit for his moves.

It is also true that the gates of the Kingdom of Heaven cannot be blown open by hydrogen bombs. But that fact does not satisfy God, and it does not satisfy us. He loves us and has set out to save us here. Jesus told us to pray, "Thy Kingdom come *on earth* as it is in heaven." Another way of saying this is, "He wants us to annex the world to heaven." Every man, woman, and child in the world who is lost or who has hate in his heart is a failure for God. No, he is a *delay* for God.

Now we are ready to see why God left His world imperfect, unfinished *until we are ready to help Him:* it is because we are being trained in this school of life to become not only sons but also fellow creators with God. This part of His universe is a joint program in which His perfection is combined with our imperfection until we learn to work with Him as members of His divine family.

So the words of Jesus, "All things are possible to him who believes," are true if we believe *long enough, intensively enough,* and if we carry that belief to the limit and *do something about it*. I think the type of religion that says, "All I have to do is pray and God will do all the rest," is wrong. He would do it all without us, if that were true.

But an opposite mistake would be to try to do it alone without God. Working *with* God, all things are possible. Working *without* God, nothing will come out right. This general truth is not enough. We need to know how to put it into practice here and now.

Here is how it can be applied. Suppose that we are to have an interview with an important person. Let us try to co-operate with God. We may say:

Lord, I am to see this man today. You have a plan in your mind for our conversation which is beyond my present understanding. Please prepare us both; prepare *him* and prepare *me* so that both of us will be following Thee. May we both agree with Thy plan. Then we will agree with one another. May we both see the importance of what we are doing as Thou dost see it. Help us to see what can be omitted. Now, Lord, I am going. Come with me, and while we are on the way, I want to do nothing, say nothing, think nothing but what Thou wantest. I want what Thou wantest. I am listening hard to hear what Thou art whispering. Speak, for Thy servant heareth.

Have you tried that? Whether it works or not depends of course on whether there is a God who answers back. Millions of people who have tried calling on Him say that He does answer. I am one of them. I witness, as millions of others do, that it makes every contact with important people better. It works so well that we are sure God was there preparing the way before us. Our experience assures us that God goes ahead and sets the stage. He is the unseen companion during the interview.

We are helping God, and He is helping us, and the two of us together are helping the world. Thus it becomes literally working *with* God.

In the last terrible week in Jesus' life He wept over Jerusalem and said, "Oh, Jerusalem, if only you knew the conditions of peace, but they are hidden from your eyes. There shall not be left one stone upon another that shall not be thrown down because you did not know the time of your visitation." God in Christ was there to save them, but they crucified Him. If Jesus wept then, He weeps now. I think we have not yet seen or followed the conditions of peace. We have thought our salvation lay in the philosophy which says, "In time of peace prepare for war." And then we got too strong or else our opponent got too strong, or we became so afraid that one of us started war. Each side is always *sure* that it was his enemy who started it.

Will God permit another world war? Nobody knows.

We have seen that God set us free because our free co-operation with Him was necessary before we could become the sons of God. God took a chance when He set us free. We *could* go to the devil instead of going to God. Thus far God has taken the risk and stayed by His daring experiment on this planet. I often wonder if He has tried this experiment and finally wiped it out in some other parts of the universe. Will He stand by it here to the point of allowing us to destroy ourselves on this planet with the Frankenstein which we have created? We just do not know. We may pray that He will intervene before we annihilate ourselves. Many Christians do pray for that, but I do not think it is what we should pray for. I think we should pray that all of us may see before it is too late that *the pathway to peace is through the love of Christ expressed in surprising kindness.*

We have discovered what love will do since we started our Point Four Program around the world. Are we going to try the way of love on a world scale? This, I think, is the only road to survival. Yet, like fools, we will spend a thousand dollars to threaten or kill for every dollar we spend to help.

Our human attempts to understand God's ways are pathetically naïve. In His sight we are perhaps no wiser than the Negro interpretation of God in "Green Pastures," which pictures God as Himself learning to use love instead of force. God has never changed like that! But our idea of Him has reformed. It is because we do not understand God that we do not help Him. Those who have seen God in the face of Jesus Christ, and who have really taken a good look at Jesus Christ, know what it means to say that "God is love." At least they know in part. But the vast majority of the human race still believes that God is marching on into one war after another, calling on the nations to destroy one another, ad infinitum!

The youth of every generation are bewildered and dismayed by this contradiction between the words they hear in church and the bloody practices of men and nations. It is hard for them to realize that mankind is still treading slowly up the road toward an understanding of Jesus. A few of these young people, thank God, see that they themselves are called to give the world a vision of Jesus as the best idea of God man has ever had.

"Green Pastures" is wrong. God is *not* improving His character. But the *idea* of God held by the human race is still on the way up. We are still learning, as Whittier said in that glorious line,

> Where Jesus knelt to share with Thee
> The silence of eternity, interpreted by love.

Helping God means that we must understand Him, what He is doing, what He likes, what He dislikes, what He is. And that means that we must walk and talk and live with Jesus daily because, as Jesus said, "He who has seen me has seen the Father."

No man ever really sees the Father except in the life of Jesus. This is exactly what Jesus said Himself, and it is true. We have seen gods, but we have not seen the Father of Love except in the face of Jesus Christ.

So we help God, first, by understanding Jesus Christ, and we help Him, second, by praying and listening.

The third way in which we help God is by helping others, asking nothing in return. The man who is helping others for a price may get the price, but he spoils the gratitude and love which would come if he had not driven his bargain. This applies to the nation as well as to the individual. America and the United Nations are launched upon a great program of helping the world. The danger is not that we shall stop. The constant temptation is that we shall ask people to pay us back by granting us special privileges. The proposal to withhold money from India because she will not join a military pact with us is bad from every viewpoint. It will punish hungry people who knew nothing about a military alliance.

There is a world of difference between those who help when their attention is called to need, and those who *go out to find need.*

Most people will help if a need is called to their attention. They let God come to them and do the asking. But the New Testament does not teach that. It says: "Go ye into all the world and preach the gospel to every creature." We must "go and teach all nations." "You shall be my witnesses to the uttermost parts of the earth." "It is not the will of my Father that one should perish."

"God desires that all men shall be saved and come to a knowledge of the truth." No man can find a word in the teachings of Jesus to agree with the motto, "All things come to those who wait," or "Serene, I fold my hands and wait." It just isn't there!

One of the most startling things Jesus ever said was said to Peter: "I give you the keys to the kingdom. Whatever you loose on earth will be loosed in heaven. Whatever you bind on earth will be bound in heaven."

That is a terrifying responsibility when you understand it. It applies to us just as it did to Peter. Everyone who is exposed to the truth of Christ holds the key for other people. The more you think about it, the more alarming it becomes. *We have to bring the truth to them or they will never get it.*

I think there is nothing in the world that bothers me more than this. I am just not worthy to be trusted with that key. I am afraid to go to the Judgment Day and have people point accusing fingers at me and say, "You held the key, and you failed to open the door for God." That is a terrifying thought! I wish there were some way to escape it, but it seems to be what the Bible says. If we could feel that only Peter had the keys, we might let Peter take the blame. It is too obvious when you think about it that it applies to us. Even if our door is open toward heaven, but closed toward people, then we have shut them out. Jesus put it positively, as well as negatively, in the end of the 25th chapter of Matthew:

"Inasmuch as ye did it to the least of these you did it to me, and inasmuch as you failed to do it to them, you failed to do it to me." And that is terrifying. But He also said this:

"Whatever measure you use for others shall be used to measure yourself."

In India there is an ancient parable which might easily have been in the Bible. A man in hell held up his hands to God and implored Him to lift him out. So God let down a huge carrot out of heaven to hell. The man grasped the leaves, but as he was being pulled out of hell people grabbed his feet and held on. A great pyramid of people was building up below him. The man looked down and was terrified. He said, "This carrot will break if these people hang on to me." He gave a vicious kick, and the carrot broke. He and all the other people fell back into hell.

If you feel as I do as you face this uncomfortable thought, you will want to say with me, "God, be merciful to me a sinner. I have failed to open the door for others. I have lacked zeal for others. I have been concerned mostly about not getting lost myself." This points the fact that the gravest sins we ever have committed are sins of omission— of *what we did not do,* of what we left undone for others.

By this measure of what we didn't do we are deep-dyed, terrible, hopeless sinners, and we must throw ourselves on the mercy of God.

In this life we are very inefficient apprentices. We are being trained to become master workmen and fellow workers with Christ in His vast enterprise. Our obligation is to do every task before us as well as we can. There used to be a settlement house called "Do Ye the Next Thing." If we do the next thing well and unselfishly, that is all God expects of us. In fact, our work with God is extremely simple. It is hard, but it is simple. It is keeping open toward God and keeping open toward people and doing the next thing that comes to be done, not worrying about the distant scene but happily doing what we can do for others every day. We should not care whether our work gets publicity or not. Every kindness is important, and everyone who does a kindness is important, because at that moment he is doing what God most wants him to do. It would be better for us to throw away ninety-nine per cent of our learning and our tangled philosophy and stick to just one simple thing for our daily life—to keep asking God, "Who needs me next, Father?" It is not necessary to look too far ahead. God is there waiting for us, and we can trust His wisdom. If we are doing something that helps people, it helps and pleases God.

We have a song in Camp Farthest Out called, "Throw It Out the Window." Throw all your problems, all your selfish seekings, all your tangled and intricate argumentation out the window, and go back to the simple life of constantly abiding and constantly helping.

We cannot keep Christ unless we give Him away. Alcoholics Anonymous know that. They are so weak that they dare not allow themselves to lose even a little ground. They keep their victory by starting at once to save other alcoholics. When the rest of us fall, our fall is not so obvious to other people as when a man gets drunk. In that respect the alcoholic has the advantage. He knows when he is lost, for he falls all the way to the bottom of the stairs. We lose our battle with the devil, and often nobody knows we lost. We can lose all our religion without going to jail or without even being censured by our neighbors. Our sin can be like a hidden, inactive cancer. It may not hurt for the moment. When it does cause us pain, it may be too late.

Many Christians are suffering from slow death of the soul because they are not helping God reach others. In non-Christian areas it is easier for the ordinary Christian to perform some kind of service than it is in this country, because in those areas the people are illiterate and eager to learn to read. They are hungry and very eager to be helped. So the Christians can teach them or help them to feed their families and thus witness at the same time.

We are not going to win this world for Christ until our clergymen get the church members out of the bleachers and into the game. You cannot have the glory until you become a channel.

It is harder to witness for Christ in America than it is in non-Christian countries. At least it was, until recently. It was not considered good taste to talk about religion, much less about Jesus Christ. But I think this has changed in the past few years, in many areas.

Many people are troubled because they do not know *how* to witness. They cannot use the language that the minister uses. Never mind; *the greatest witness is kindness and helpfulness.* If you pray for others enough and love them enough they will not need words. In the heart of every man and woman there is some need, a longing to be understood, or some other need. It would be good for every Christian to read Dale Carnegie's *How to Win Friends and Influence People.* We might also study the techniques of Alcoholics Anonymous, for they have learned how to win their man. They wait patiently for months, until some day, when their man is thoroughly disgusted with his debauchery and, like the Prodigal Son, is ready to go home, they come and lead him by the hand back to the Father. So if any man tells you he is miserable and wants the secret of the happy life, say to him, "Start today saying silently, 'God, I want to help You. What can I do for You? Whom can I help You with?' "

Isaiah 6 records a wonderful vision in which he saw the Lord "high and lifted up on a throne." And he heard a voice saying, "Whom shall I send? Who will go for us?" And Isaiah answered, "Here am I; send me."

That is what God is looking for—people who will pray until God speaks and then will say, "Here am I; send me."

People who say that they have not studied the science of reaching people and do not know the techniques about "saying the right words" need not worry. The right words do not matter; it is the right spirit that counts. Even if you stumble and stammer and don't say anything that is persuasive, those in need will catch your spirit. Love will convince them far more than a thousand words or even a thousand pages. If we have all the techniques in the world but lack love, we are like a cracked bell. And people see through the imitation; they see the crack.

The viewpoint in this chapter and in this book is high and beautiful, but it is not easy to hold. There is a constant downward drag by the practices and the viewpoints of people in our selfish world. In every situation in which we try to be different from others there is a spiritual warfare between us and them. Either we lift them up, or they drag us down.

And so this practice of lifting people to God has got to be intense and energetic and constant. If we have one hundred friends who are hostile to it, that means that our zeal must be one hundred times as great for our way of life as theirs. And it must have no exception. When we are in God's service, it is fatal for us to allow ourselves to be frustrated by one little weakness or by one little failure of others to return our love.

Above all, we must be interested in the *whole* of a man's life. We dare not say, "I am interested in your soul, but not in the rest of you." We must be interested in all that everybody is doing, is saying, is hoping, or our negatives will cancel out all the good that we are trying to do.

XIV

HOW WE CAN SAVE THE WORLD

WE USED TO BE TOLD THAT OSTRICHES HIDE THEIR HEADS IN the sand when they hear the lions roar. It is now denied that ostriches ever really did this. But many *human* ostriches hide their heads when danger is near, and just try to forget it! They are foolish.

Equally foolish are those who wring their hands in despair.

It is terribly wrong for us to think we have nothing to do—no part to play.

It is also wrong to say that "somehow" everything is *sure* to come out all right. I say it is *not* sure to come out all right. I say it depends on what we (all of us) do about it.

Preachers always have been tempted to say, "Peace, peace," when there was no peace. Their congregations *want a sense of security*. Never in history has a nation made creature comfort its passion as much as we do now in the U.S.A. And preachers today find that the temptation to keep their congregations comfortable is stronger than ever before. Today it is the scientists and the military men who are sounding the prophetic warnings.

When the atom bomb first appeared, and our great scientists told us what an appalling threat hung over our heads, we were really frightened. Then we all asked, "What can we do?" Among most people that terror is beginning to disap-

177

pear. We are getting accustomed to peril as people become accustomed to living near a volcano. Perhaps the most dangerous state of mind is that in which we are plunged right now: "Nothing has happened so far, so perhaps it won't."

I think it would be a tragedy for the human race to get over its fear of the atom bomb and settle back into the old rut. For that old rut can lead our world to annihilation. The thoughts and plans of men around the world are at cross purposes with the plans of God. Men have turned God's gifts into poison. The threat of immediate conflict seems not to be as great as it was four years ago, yet doom hangs over us just as truly as it did then. That doom will come sooner or later unless we can lift our low standards of social morality. We have got to find a new rut, and fast!

Opposition to such reform does not come entirely from evil men. Some very devout people find this threat of doom corroborating their theology. Some even say that the worse we get, the sooner Christ will return. They wait for Christ to appear on the clouds in the air when things get bad enough!

Others think that "it is all in the hands of God." They can look on calmly while He saves His world or destroys it, as He desires.

One man told me he had made his peace with God—"So let it come."

Still others are whistling in an attempt to conceal their secret fear.

But the largest number have put their faith in "meeting force with force, and gun with gun, and bomb with bomb." "An eye for an eye and a tooth for a tooth," the Old Testament called it. The theory is that if we have a larger pile of bombs than the enemy we shall frighten them into refraining from attack.

None of these points of view will save the world. The

only people who can do anything for our age are those *who know what to do and do it.*

Do we know what to do? We have seen that the cause of our present peril is a far deeper fear than is commonly supposed. No one is more zealous than I to accomplish political and social reforms, and yet I know perfectly well that this alone will not solve our problems. I think social reforms are necessary, but I am sure they are not enough.

You may set up a perfect political system in any country, but if the people are unworthy the system breaks down. Our democracy is unquestionably the best government in the world if it is carried on by good people, but it is far and away the most difficult system in the world to work successfully—because every man must rule. A helicopter gets us around much more rapidly and efficiently than walking, but if we do not know how to run it, the helicopter is a menace instead of a help. Democracy is like that. It is a good thing if the people are ready for it, but most democracies around the world have been failing: they have failed because their people lacked character and public spirit and education.

If we are to survive with our inconceivably dangerous atomic power we have got to change the thought, and will and character of the world. It isn't enough to change the wills and thoughts of Americans. We have got to work *all over the planet with the entire human race.* If we can't do that we are doomed. At best, we shall only postpone doomsday. Meanwhile we must tremble under an armed, uneasy truce.

A generation ago, people were saying, "You can't change human nature." But now we know better. It *can* be changed. Thank God, that is easier to change than anything else in the universe, because it is so incredibly impressionable. Infinitesimal electric currents which the most delicate machines can barely *detect* are impressing and changing the cortex of our brains all the time. If our brains required as much energy as ordinary telephone wires, it would take more energy to run one brain than to supply all the electrical energy used in New York City. The brain is that delicate. Evil men made use of that fact first. They did it with scientific propaganda. I have heard good Christians oppose propaganda on the ground that it "invaded personality." But what is the Gospel if it is not propaganda?

/.   One thing is clear that we must do. We must release a sufficient volume of *the right kind of propaganda* not only to counteract the evil propaganda all about us, but to build up a great reservoir of good thinking and of good will. Only thus can the world be saved.

We could have done this sooner if we had been interested. But we did not realize how important it was. We were not earnest enough about saving the world; we were obsessed with making money. We Christians today must therefore confess our responsibility for the world's failure. While we slumbered, other people were hard at work. While we failed to go all out in spreading the Christian Gospel, energetic evangelists of a false materialistic gospel *have* gone all out to sow their ideas everywhere. Not only did we not sow our ideas; we failed also to live up to them.

Our sin has found us out. It is time for us to repent. But repentance merely in words is a fraud. Repentance really means turning around and going the other way. That would be sufficient if we went the other way fast enough.

What is the matter with our Christianity? We have watered down the high summons of Jesus until it sounds like a lazy, good-natured, but utterly selfish, philosophy of "mind your own business." We were able to do this because a large section of the churches came to believe that only a part of the Bible was true, and we chose the part that suited our own predilection! Many of us doubted that there was a future life, and many, many doubted that the way of salvation described in the Bible was true.

So we became obsessed with our own salvation and with our own comfort here, and we gave little thought for the salvation of the rest of the world, either here or hereafter.

We must change before it is too late. Fortunately, the world was never in such a state of receptivity to the idea of change as it is now. A hundred factors have all pulled the world together and made it think as one world. It *is* becoming one world, in spite of the iron curtain. The airplane and the radio, the steamship, the automobile, the motion picture, the tourists, perhaps above all *the soldiers* who have gone into all the countries where wars have taken place, have helped in this. And Communist propaganda, too, has had a mighty influence. All of these things have aroused in the common people of the world a great longing to come up out of their poverty. In all past ages they lived in a state of sullen despair. They were fatalists. Their own religions taught them to be submissive in the hope that in another incarnation they would be in a better state. Now they see that fatalism is not the answer, and they are demanding better conditions of life. Their sullen submission has changed to a grim determination to catch up with the rest of us. This was seen in the recent uprising in Iran. Big landowners chased the Shah of Iran out, but the little people rose and revolted against their own landholders, and the Shah came back as a defender of the little people.

It was good that the President of the United States saw this "handwriting on the wall." It was good that the President and our Congress promised that we would help the world out of its present hunger and misery by sharing our technical knowledge. It is a happy thing, too, that the United Nations followed this lead of America, and that a great effort is now being made to improve economic conditions all over the world. This is good and it is exciting. But as everybody will admit, *it isn't enough.*

There must also be a mighty spiritual rebirth of the world, and this is something that neither our government nor any other government can bring about. Only the missionaries have a gospel that can change human nature. They and they alone have been doing this in all parts of the world. The government itself would be the first to admit that its representatives are seldom equipped to change the spiritual climate of the countries into which they go.

This means that the Church must revive its missionary interest. It ought to spend a billion dollars on foreign missions. It should send a very large number of technically trained men who also have great spiritual power. It should train an even larger number of nationals and give them financial aid. If the Church is going to do this it must change its present attitude. Church members spent 29 cents less per year per capita for foreign missions in 1953 than they spent in 1913. That means that we have lost interest in foreign missions. And this, I think, is the most tragic mistake we have made in the world today. At the very moment when the world needs most desperately the very thing that the church can give, the Church has failed to give it!

The governments are ahead of the Church in their interest in lifting the masses of humanity out of misery. Why the Church is so blind is a highly controversial question. Perhaps it is for a number of reasons. Anthropologists have led a great many educated people to believe that the religion of primitive peoples is so intertwined with their customs that changing it may do them real harm. A large number of Christians are suffering from what Dr. L. P. Jacks calls "the lost radiance of the Christian religion." He says we have so lost the Pentecostal power of the Early Church that with our millions of members today we cannot do what a few thousand were able to do in the first and second centuries. We have been suffering from a creeping spiritual paralysis. This has been accompanied by doubt concerning Jesus Christ, and about our own religion. The doubt has increased the paralysis, and the paralysis has injured Christian missions.

But a revival is beginning to sweep through the country, and there is already some improvement evident in foreign missions. The foreign mission enterprise is sending more doctors and agricultural experts and other social service men, proportionately, than it did before. These are all good signs. The only trouble is that the upturn is dangerously slow in a crisis in which the world needs speed and power.

The government is carrying on work that the Church ought to be carrying on. It is doing this because it must be done. Point IV, thus far, is almost wholly a government project. If the Church did what Point IV is doing, the Church could do it more efficiently and at far less cost. The program would be manned by men with Christian motives, and with an evangelistic fervor, as well as with technical skill. But so long as the church fails to see this vision and do it the government must carry on.

There is only one way to break the Church out of its present vicious circle. That is for a large number of Christian people to see the vision, to agitate within their own churches.

These are the things we can do:

1. We can become earnest students of world need, and can get other people in our churches to study world need. I mean missions not only as they now are, but as they ought to be. We will also study the other organizations that are trying to meet those needs.

2. We can pray and we can form prayer cells to pray for the people who are trying to meet world need. We can

pray for all those who need our prayers, both in government, and in the church, and in business.

We can pray and then write kindly, helpful letters. We can set aside a definite time each day, perhaps our devotional hour, to pray for individuals and to write to them.

3. We can help greatly expand the foreign missions program of our own church and denomination, especially in the direction of sending technologically trained missionaries. We can write to the heads of our denomination, urging them to devote a larger proportion of the church giving to foreign missions. We can develop special projects for raising money for missions in our Sunday school and in the church. We can see that a larger percentage of our church's giving goes to foreign missions. We can make it our goal that 50 per cent of our church's income should go for benevolences, and that 50 per cent of the benevolence money should go to the foreign field. We can agitate for tithing so as to help meet this need. We can suggest that war bonds be converted into peace bonds by giving them for this program. Briefly, we can inspire the church to *action*.

4. We can finance nationals both in this country and abroad.

"Awake" is being promoted by Koinonia in Baltimore. The letters of "Awake" stand for "America's War of Amazing Kindness Everywhere." That is the kind of war that the Church ought to be waging on a big scale. It is waging that war on a small scale through CARE and Church World Service and other organizations which are sending food and clothing abroad. All are doing a great deal of good. But they are stop-gap emergency measures. The hungry people of the world want *more than charity*, they want to *be helped to help themselves*. They want to be able to raise bigger crops on their land; they want land of their own; they want credit banks so that they can borrow money without paying terrible rates of interest. They want to get rid of disease. Help them to help themselves. This is what the Church ought to be doing *on a very large scale*. And this is what the Church *will do* just as soon as enough people, like you and myself, work to change its present attitude of lethargy.

If the Church would Awake, and respond to this gigantic world need which is now so pressing in Asia and Africa and Latin America, I am sure that for the first time in world history we could bring the world to Christ. Early in this century John R. Mott challenged the student world with his slogan—"The Evangelization of the World in This Generation." Mott was two generations ahead of his time. It could not be done in his day. Communication was too poor. It took Mott many months to go around the world by steamship. Today one can go around the world by air; it is no uncommon thing for church leaders to travel around the world two or three times in one year. With literacy and simple reading it is possible to reach millions and millions more people than we were able to reach a few years ago. By means of the radio one can speak to the end of the world.

The world is like an overripe fruit. It is going to be evangelized to *something*. If Christianity is not energetic enough and virile enough to capture the world, something else will be. It may be Communism. And if all the Communists were destroyed some other idea would come to take Communism's place, because these multitudes of people around the world, who up to this time have been asleep in despair, are reaching up their hands for somebody to help them. Whoever helps them can win their hearts. Our hydrogen bombs and atom bombs cannot prevent these nations from *voting* Communist, but whoever convinces them that he is their friend can win their hearts. The new nationalist countries are suspicious of people who spend their time only on evangelism, but they are very enthusiastic about men who help them with their great needs—food, health and literacy. If the Christians do help them adequately there will be little or no need for propaganda for Christianity. The people will want to be Christians because Christianity does so much for them. They will be seekers; it will not be necessary to pursue them.

You and I as Christians need some simple formula for daily living that will hold us to our task within our community and also around the world. Is there such a formula? After a lifetime of labor, Einstein has formulated an equation which describes the behavior of all our physical world. Can we write a formula which will describe our best way of living day by day as a Christian?

I propose this. It is so simple that a little child can understand it and do it. Its only defect is that it is so simple that educated people may think it is beneath their dignity. Here is the formula: The soul will have one hand reaching to the sky asking: "Father, how can I help you help your world?" and will listen for His reply. The other hand will reach down and out to humanity all around the world, asking, "Everybody, everywhere, how can I help you?" Wide open, *upward* all the time—and wide open outward all the time. It is allowing ourselves to be a wide-open channel, ever widening as God stretches us. Minute by minute we do the thing that comes to us, not worrying about the future.

If we live this way, the sum total of our years will be enormously beneficial, and we shall be happy because we shall be free from worry. We throw away the multitudinous, useless, and often harmful habits that would encumber us, and live a simple life—simple as a pipe line between God and the world.